Return from Berlin

Return from Berlin

The Eye of a Navigator

Robert Grilley

Pen & Sword
AVIATION

First published in Great Britain in 2005 by
PEN & SWORD AVIATION
an imprint of
Pen & Sword Books Limited
47 Church Street
Barnsley
South Yorkshire
S70 2AS

ISBN 1 84415 214 6

Published in the USA by
The University of Wisconsin Press

A CIP catalogue record for this book
is available from the British Library.

Printed and bound in Great Britain by
CPI UK

Pen & Sword Books Ltd incorporates the imprints of
Pen & Sword Aviation, Pen & Sword Maritime, Pen & Sword Military,
Wharncliffe Local History, Pen & Sword Select,
Pen & Sword Military Classics and Leo Cooper.

For a complete list of Pen & Sword titles please contact:
PEN & SWORD BOOKS LIMITED
47 Church Street, Barnsley, South Yorkshire, S70 2AS, England.
E-mail: enquiries@pen-and-sword.co.uk
Website: www.pen-and-sword.co.uk

With deepest affection, I dedicate this book to the young men who flew with me through the flak-filled skies over Nazi Germany fifty-nine years ago. They were brave beyond measure, filled with unwarranted optimism and high spirits. They were smart and good-looking and regarded each other with that special friendship known only to combat soldiers.

And yet, even as I reflect on their virtues, it's clear that these intrepid members of my B-17 crew and I survived only because our lottery tickets in that game of life and death turned out to be winners, so we were among those who came home to grow old slowly, fulfilling Nature's original intentions for us.

Contents

Contents

Illustrations

Photographs

Acknowledgments

For a beginner at my advanced age, a book is an awesome project. I have an unusually clear long-term memory and exceptional things to remember, but to cause a book to become more than an fanciful daydream today, one needs the computer skills I've never learned.

Fortunately, my daughter Juneko; my son Rob; and my busy scientist wife, Ei Terasawa; could type for me. In particular, Ei, in spite of her long hours devoted to neuroscience research, and the necessary world travel pertinent to it, was willing to make it all work for me, that is, the transformation of my Spencerian hand into neat manuscript on pages and disks; and often when I'd thought I'd said it right, I tended to change my mind. For this she never seemed to lose patience. And, although they live far away, my daughter Rinelda and son Dorian have shown their enthusiasm for and pride in the book.

Also, I must thank my editor Erin Holman for keeping her cool in the face of my sometimes intransigent moods.

Then too, my peer readers, with their wonderfully complimentary words recommending approval of the book, brought joy to my heart. They are Bruce Murray and Harold Scheub of the University of Wisconsin–Madison and Joseph Smith of the University of Chicago, an Englishman who likes my prose.

Return from Berlin

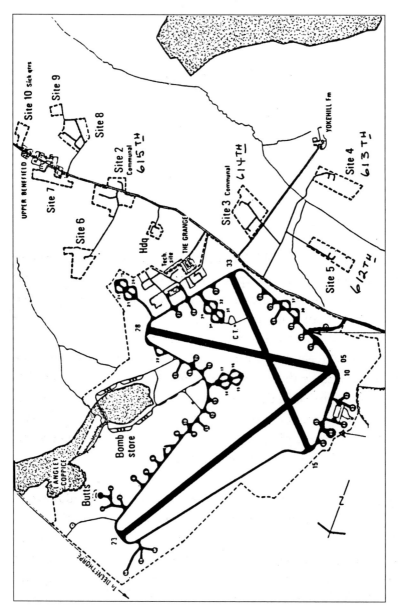

Deenethorpe. Sta. 128

Prologue

Robert Earl Grilley got his draft number and induction notice in short sequence. He was exceptionally physical, so before you could say Jack Robinson, or more timely, Jack Pershing, he'd easily passed muster, and began studying war as a doughboy at Camp Grant in Rockford—close order drill with a Springfield rifle out in the hot sun in a khaki woolen uniform. Then suddenly, just before he shipped overseas with the 32d Red Arrow Division, he and his Ella Louise were married in the camp chapel. I don't know whether they had time and place for consummation. Mother never talked about such things, but she did say, more than once, that he clung awfully tight to her until moments before he had to leave.

During the Argonne campaign in 1918, the exact date is unknown to me, my brave doughboy father was cut down by mortar fire and smothered in mustard gas. It was nip and tuck, but he made it through with a measure of true grit, and our thin thread of life was preserved. Thus, after the long convalescence, my begetting was safely accomplished, and I was born, a seven pound, twelve ounce, chronically happy child in Lancaster, Wisconsin, early on Sunday morning, November 14, 1920.

Robert Earl Grilley, my brave doughboy father, 1917.

In fact, as I understand it, I was so unaccountably happy, even in the beginning, that my very well-educated mother could not have been blamed if she suspected, for only the briefest moment, that I might be slightly simple. However, in the unlikely event that such a notion ever occurred to her, it would have been fleeting, and as things came into focus for me, I was assured that she considered me to be a future prodigy.

Of course happiness, like beauty, is a matter of perception, and my mother was a mistress of illusion, so when I was young, very young, the sweet birds sang in spite of hard times and our particular condition, a dying father and more-than-occasional spells of genteel poverty.

I got off to a good start though, and hadn't the slightest hint until I was four that some degree of privation could be common; and even after the blow fell, the first crisis you might call it, my playful indolence simply changed to a travel and adventure mode. But thinking back about it, I can say that mother had remarkable self-control and kept from me whatever forebodings she must have felt in the face of such a calamity, and prepared for the trip as if we were going on vacation.

But, long before it ever came to that, when I was first learning the rudiments of life, she told me, as her closest confidant, that my father had been hurt in the war, although not too badly, and that by then he was well again and everything would be all right. For sure, it seemed to be. We lived in a big white house, and I had ice cream often. Mamma played with me a lot and sang "Listen to the mocking bird, listen to the mockingbird," and I would listen and sometimes hear a robin high in the elm tree where I couldn't see him, or maybe just sparrows bickering in the vines, but when we sat out on the porch after supper there'd be a mourning dove calling when it was getting dark. It sounded like he was asking someone a question over and over again.

That was before we had a radio, and Mamma often sang songs she learned when she was a little girl, mostly from her grandfather

Cruger in Waterloo, who had been shot in the Civil War fighting to free the slaves but who was still, in spite of it all, happy as the day was long. She was awfully proud of him, and never tired of telling that he went on to become justice of the peace and to teach people how to behave themselves and get along with each other. His closest friend was also a "man of peace," as Mamma would say, a Catholic priest; but though he, her grandpa, was a strict Methodist, they never ever argued about what Jesus was supposed to have said. They were true Christians.

The calamity I spoke of, which in effect, sent us off by railroad pass to live with relatives in gulf-coast Texas, was my father's sudden relapse, a bloody lung hemorrhage that necessitated a medical leave without pay, forcing him back to the Veterans' Hospital, for God only knew how long.

We could have gone to Deerfield to stay with Grandpa and Grandma, a humiliating prospect, but Mamma thought the Texas option would, since it was expected to be short term, be very educational for me.

At this point mother saw fit to fill out the story a little more. They had been married in Rockford after he'd been drafted, and she came back to teach in a country school. He was sent to fight in France, and wounded and gassed in the Argonne Forest, but she said, "Daddy is strong. He'll get well, don't worry." She was proud and a little sad; both. "Only the good men went, while the slackers stayed home and made big money." Sometimes she'd get carried away and say that he was shell-shocked too, which gave him bad headaches. "No man should be asked to go over to France and fight for a country that didn't care about him. If it did, the government would do something for his family."

But then she'd cheer up and tell me that in no time he'd be out of the hospital and the railroad would give him back his job. They were saving it for him because he had earned "rights" in the years that he'd worked for them before the war. They'd even given him credit for the time he served in the army. So some people did care about what he did for his country.

Years passed and up I grew. For a while, my father was supported by a gradually descending series of railroad sinecures, until finally, his employers lost patience, and he was given no choice but to retire to a veterans' hospital, where he died.

His last trivial job had been in Madison. We moved there when I was eight, and Mamma solemnly declared, "Come what may, as long as I can stand on my own two feet and hold my head up, this will be where you'll go to school."

No doubt, Madison was "where it was at." It had long been known as the Athens of the Midwest, and the Great Depression had scarcely touched it. Mamma's first job was coloring black-and-white portrait photos for the Badger Studio, a practice she found distastefully lowbrow, but with that to supplement a pittance the government doled out in recognition of my father's sacrifice, we could get by until something more suitable could be found.

She was still youthful and good looking. Her dietary deprivation had, if anything, trimmed her figure, and clarified her chin and cheekbones, so it was not surprising that with a stylish new dress as an advance on her wage, she landed a job as a saleslady at Simpson's, the city's most exclusive women's store, and after that, we turned the corner, no longer abject. Mamma could hold her head up high.

It was a lovely time and place to be a kid, but I don't remember being pampered, only richly appreciated, with affirmative hugs now and then. There were always coins for serious things; model airplane materials, quality drawing paper, books and magazines, and without question, the less serious, but soul-gratifying necessities like Saturday movie matinees at the Majestic, a dime a kid, with giant double Milky Ways handed out to grasping little hands by uniformed ushers to get us out of the place before 5:00 P.M., making way for the twenty-five-cent patrons; then the two block run at full speed to burn some of our joyous, ineluctable energy, and the walk home, giggling and jostling with my neighborhood pal, chewing great chunks of candy that would in no way spoil my supper of Campbell's pork and beans with fried potatoes and a helping of boiled greens to keep my bowels open, and a tall glass of milk, so creamy it gurgled voluptuously when poured from the bottle.

After that, the Saturday night mystery on our Gothic window-shaped Philco gave zest to the evening.

From one happy year to the next, we seemed to go with the flow, while my mother brought intuitive order to things. Her plans were so inconspicuous that, if noticed at all, they appeared to be simply the work of Providence.

It could never be said though that she had even the slightest disingenuous thought in her pretty head, but she always kept an eye open for something that might turn out to be useful in the long run, so when I was enthusiastically involved in the Children's Creative Art School during several summers circa 1931–32, taught by Della Wilson, professor of art education at the University of Wisconsin, Mother formed a warm friendship with her, and kept it warm over the years. It was in no way deceitful. I'm sure they really found each other to be kindred souls, with conservative views on art; and too, they each had someone to look after: Della, her old mother, and Mamma, me. So, one shouldn't be at all surprised that a few years later, Miss Wilson was able to do me a favor.

Mother bided her time regarding art until my senior year, when she used her long-standing friendship with Miss Wilson to gain an acquaintance with Professor Roland Stebbins, a gallant old Bostonian with a twinkle in his eye, and a master of life drawing. We were invited out to his place for dinner to meet his wife, Hortie.

We charmed them, and soon I was invited to sit in on his life class, and the rest, as the old cliché goes, is history. I should add, that Stebbie observed, after a few sessions, that I had an eye like a musician has an ear.

Prologue

When I made the awesome transition to university, I left behind all vestiges of childhood, which Mother's loving care had tended to prolong. We became hard-working partners, as equals. I gave up the very large, seven-day-a-week newspaper route I'd carried like a sturdy donkey, and got a twenty hour a week job in the paint and wallpaper department of a large hardware store and set out to work my way through college.

The ambience was glorious; a place known round the world; gold and silver there for the taking; art and art history, and new loves in English and European history, botany and zoology, even a slight touch of genetics (Gregor Mendel's sweet peas), primitive by modern standards, but mind-opening. I found teachers who still come back to me. Among them was Helen C. White, for whom the library of the University of Wisconsin is named. I had a year's senior writing seminar with her, where she taught me to listen to the music of language.

In 1940, during my second year at the University of Wisconsin, the federal government offered an extensive flying training program to fifty students who could qualify by passing thorough physical and written examinations, and interview. This seemed quite miraculous to me, and I was astonished to be chosen. It was called Civilian Pilot Training (CPT) and was undoubtedly a thinly veiled preparedness measure to be given at all large universities. The CPT was presented in three stages: primary, after which we received a pilot's license; secondary in aerobatics; and finally, cross-country, a brief introduction to instrument flying.

I began pilot training with an already well-developed understanding of aerodynamic theory, and fortunately my first instructor—a mild-mannered, nearly middle-aged man who in no way resembled my preconceived image of a flier—showed me with bemused tolerance the considerable difference between theory and practice. I've kept a place in my heart for him ever since. His name was Mike Miller. He taught me the fundamentals of flight that have lasted a lifetime.

The newly begun war in Europe still seemed remote, but one of my art professors was skeptical about our neutrality.

"You'll be flying over Berlin before long, and shot at," he remarked without a trace of humor.

I laughed, but the next two years were short, and after my graduation I offered myself as an aviation cadet. My mother, a patient optimist but long-suffering World War I widow, presented the truth, though not insistently, that my university-confirmed professional standing in art would surely entitle me to some type of technical placement. I would have none of it, and she was surprisingly willing to accept it with grace.

I was readily taken as a cadet, although the pipeline was anything but direct. Our involvement in the war had happened so quickly that the Air Force was not prepared to process and train the thousands of willing young hopefuls, and all but the earliest enlistees were sent off to holding programs, starting with Army Infantry Basic Training and, after that, to College Training Detachments for two months for touches of math, geography, and English, the latter to polish off the rough edges of those who might be expected to become officers and gentlemen.

I was pleased to be sent to Western Reserve University in Cleveland, and I have happy memories of that assignment. It was not more than a few steps from a world-class art museum and the great Cleveland Symphony, and the good-natured old nonprofessional second lieutenant in charge of my detachment was happy to see me engage in such cultural interests on Sunday afternoons.

It was early spring of 1943 when I arrived at the classification center in Nashville, Tennessee, with a mixed group of men and boys to be sifted and winnowed, where the Air Force could finally take the measure of what they'd accumulated. We were to be separated as pilot, navigator, or bombardier trainees, or none of the three. A great number were found unsuitable and dropped—sent to Biloxi, a heartless and extravagant process.

Myself as an aviation cadet, spring 1943.

After the final and notably redundant academic and physical exams, we were given a strange new one called Aptitude Rating for Military Aeronautics (ARMA), a psychological exam. I have no recollection of the doctors' questions or of our discussion, but they were perfectly satisfied with my response and indicated it to be the case with their signatures. I'd be interested after all these years to magically hear a playback of that interview to find out what it was they were after.

When all things were taken into account, I was told I would be a navigator, which caught me totally by surprise. Was I not already a CPT-trained pilot with more than 200 hours in my log book? I vigorously complained to the most available officer in charge of proceedings, who was not at all irritated by my insubordination. He calmly congratulated me for having done very well in all categories of the exams and simply, with obvious finality, repeated that I would be, in his judgment, an excellent navigator. He added, for further clarification, that there was already a long backlog of cadets waiting for openings in pilot primary schools and that my overall familiarity with maps and flying would give me a head start in air navigation.

I was outraged! Swore a blue streak on my way back to the barracks. But the pique passed in a short time, and I actually learned to love my new area of flying expertise, which I considered splendidly arcane.

I graduated well up in my cadet class, with a commission as a second lieutenant, and moved on to B-17 crew formation and operational training at Ellsworth Field near Rapid City, South Dakota, and in a stroke of good fortune, I found that I'd joined one of the finest, bravest bunch of young men the Air Force had so far assembled. I hadn't the slightest reservation about going to war with them, but when we entered into the biggest fight in human history, there were many times when it seemed that a second case of nip and tuck in my family might occur. We very nearly met our match, yet the right prevailed at inestimable cost. My flak suit held though, and our family DNA was preserved with none of my father's misfortune.

Prologue

Our crew in training at Rapid City, South Dakota, January 1944. *Back row, from left:* Jay Karper, Larry Million, Porter Ham, Russell Lockhart, and Ray Miller. *Front row:* Grilley, Lloyd Null, Elno Pyles, and Otto Schlaegel.

In the fall of 1945, having gotten back to the real world, I painted a little English landscape with a B-17 on landing approach from which a red flare arches back in a graceful curve. Its thin trace of scarlet is a fine accent against the dramatic sky, but to the medics its message was that there were wounded on board. I called the picture *Return from Berlin.*

It might well have been *Return from Ludwigshafen,* except on that trip we very nearly bought the farm and didn't make it all the way back to Deenethorpe. Or it could have been *Return from Merseburg,* the huge Leüna synthetic oil plant, Germany's most fiercely defended target; or it could have been Hamburg or Leipzig. But Berlin was way out ahead in symbolic meaning and was an obvious choice for a title. Even battle-tested veterans spoke of it in awe, and called it Big B. When you came back from Berlin, it was like stealing home in the World Series.

After making this subtle little war icon, I got on with my newly allotted lifetime as an artist and teacher and thought less and less

13

Yokehill Farm, July 1994. I am very grateful to Friends of the 8th Peter Wood and Herbert Watson, for giving Ei, Juneko (at left), and this old soldier a tour of the 401st site on the fiftieth anniversary of that memorable summer—1944.

about that strange martial adventure until, for a long while, it nearly vanished from my consciousness—put away, for the most part, in an unused closet of my mind.

A half-century passed, and during a nostalgic visit to England on the way back from a European tour, I was taken by two members of the Friends of the 8th Air Force organization to Deenethorpe, the base site of the 401st Bomb Group that was by then in a modern state of ruins, and to Yokehill Farm. It was by chance on the fiftieth anniversary of my first mission to Merseburg, and a flood of memories was released, as in a wide screen movie, and with them came the need to put some down on paper.

Back in my studio, as I remember it now, I look with a new compelling interest at the things on a wall reserved for images and relics

Friend of the 8th Peter Wood, myself, and Herbert Watson at the 401st monument, July 1994. Ruins of the flight control tower can be seen in the upper right corner of the photo.

from that ancient time and place; crew pictures, combat medals and such, but especially at the grainy blowup of my twenty-three-year-old predecessor in his proudly worn fifty-mission crush with its rakish tilt, a big-deal first louie with five o'clock shadow after an eight-and-a-half hour sortie on top of a four-hour prep, showing not the least signs of stress.

He regards me with an insouciant grin. "How ya doing, old Buddy?" he asks, as if to shake my hand, and suggests that I try to make an arrangement with Mephistopheles for a day or two of youth, and go with him on one more mission to Merseburg or Berlin, and then, with time and energy left over, do a drawing of Elizabeth on fine off-white handmade paper from Winsor & Newton of London.

So, to what can we attribute this insouciance? It's also there in his other postmission pictures. Was he simply a callow youngster playing war? No, on the contrary, he was a well-educated young man with structured plans for the future.

Myself after a long mission, August 1944.

Brave? Well, yes, but what does that mean? Probably he'd reached the magical assumption of invulnerability that effective combat soldiers held for as long as needed, all part of his ARMA, otherwise he'd have to have been suicidal, and our culture didn't ask outright for that—no kamikazes—but the military planners did think in terms of acceptable losses, though not within his earshot.

And then too, it was summer; one of the loveliest summers you could imagine, and the living was easy between missions. The grass was green as you'll ever see, and the sky a bright cerulean. That time, May through September, was the best you could ask for to fight with such an old-fashioned air war. He didn't have to muck about like the poor guys who did it in winter. Even the food was good—the best he'd ever had, an enormous improvement over his fare as an impoverished student. The 8th Air Force even had its own ice cream factory.

The 401st Bomb Group (H) in England at War

Deenethorpe. If you were writing a fictional work, could you have invented a more English name for a small village in the Rockingham Forest? Not likely. Sometimes I try to picture it in my mind's eye, although I never saw it. When I got there in May 1944, its stones lay scattered among tall weeds, and Deenethorpe had come to mean the 401st Bomb Group.

The village, as a community, probably reached back to the time of the Danelaw and remained essentially unchanged in the last several hundred years, until December 5, 1943, when an overloaded B-17 faltered on takeoff and crashed into its midst. This occasioned two distinct miracles. None of the crew was killed, and a peculiar quirk of nature allowed ten minutes for the houses to be evacuated before the bombs in the stillburning plane blew.

Such close proximity of towns and farms to airbases was a hazardous necessity—no wasted space. Like pieces of a jigsaw puzzle, our runways and structures were snugly fitted into these bucolic settings.

We came to the 401st as names on pulp-paper orders specifying the 613th Squadron as our military home. It sprawled across a low hill half a mile south of the threshold of runway 33, and a narrow gravel trail ran up to it from the paved Oundle to Weldon road, which was to be our main thoroughfare. The truck that took us up the eroded path at more than necessary speed dumped us off at squadron headquarters for a quick check-in by commander Major Eric de Jonckheere's sidekick, then unloaded us and our gear seemingly at random, in officer crews of four to quarters, which consisted of a semi-cylindrical Nissen hut bolted to a concrete slab. It was adequate in space for eight, and there was a crew already living there. But they were not at home at the time, maybe on a mission? I don't remember. In fact, I no longer have a memory of them at all, so soon did they disappear, maybe killed in action (KIA) prisoners of war (POW) or the last sad category, missing in action (MIA), which meant nobody knew what happened to them.

A few days after the nameless crew was gone and their belongings were packed off, we were joined by old friends, that is, old Air Force school buddies, pilot Ken Murgatroyd, copilot Jim Pennoyer, navigator Owen Jorgenson, and bombardier John Elderkin. Our pilot, Russ Lockhart, had gone through flight training with Ken, and I had been through navigation school with Jorgenson. We had arrived in England and been together at the replacement center. That they were sent to the 401st and 613th a week or so later was a pleasant coincidence.

But that's slightly ahead of my narrative, so let me get back to living conditions in a Nissen. The beds and mattresses seemed substantial, but there was only a vague promise of bedding as it turned out, available primarily through a casual black market for ragged, unlaundered sheets and natural-colored English army blankets that smelled stronger than the sheep they came from. But even so, a rather new officer and gentleman could get used to things quickly. Actually, we were the not-even-slightly-threadbare aristocrats of the military, better off by far than the mud-spattered grunts in the infantry. In my case, a little comfortable disorder would be preferable to barracks living as a cadet, where a chicken ninety-day wonder could gig you and ruin your already sparse weekend if his coin didn't bounce six inches up from your tightly made bed.

After I claimed a bunk and stashed my things, I took a walk in the lane that ran through our squadron area and past the big stone buildings labeled Yokehill Farm on the map. The Old World was out there somewhere not too far to find someday: the sixteenth century, maybe the fifteenth, damp with ivy, where the White and Red Roses had strutted and jousted and made war that was invigorating, honorable, and absolute in resolving questions of doctrine and power. So maybe a quick trip to Bosworth Field would be worthwhile on a day off after I got into the rhythm of things.

Earlier in life I had traveled to Texas and California, but in a sense I'd never really been very far from home. England was a long way away, a mythical place where beauty, age, and death commingled. A century was an eye's wink, and the salt-textured stones in churchyards were weathered long before Washington made foreigners out of us. And there was a familiarity with the sounds of English; it was different, but pleasingly so, from what we had made of it.

Here we were then, in this fabled land on the great adventure of our lives; for some of us it would never be completed. Solipsisms were thin protection, though for the most part we believed them. How else could old men persuade the young to do such things? Grant at the Wilderness showed Lincoln that pain and death (someone else's) were not demonstrable deterrents. There were moments, though, when even the toughest among us paused between swigs down at the club to hear the distant sounds of mortality hissing in his ear.

Our immediate enterprise would be operational training, the catechism of combat flying according to the 8th Air Force and, in particular, its refinements as practiced by the 401st. We burned a lot of gasoline and calories, and still there was time left over. While some used this gift from the powers above to sack in until chow, and then be off to the club to chug-a-lug, I, though by no means an abstainer, found this place too good to waste. There was a perfect Constable sketch out there or, better yet, a Bonington, if one could be located. Crazy, you might say, to be an artist gone to war while all the art people he knew were non-coms back at Fort Belvoir, Virginia, a short bus ride from The National Gallery, drawing tech manuals nine to five weekdays.

In addition to landscaping, I was an enthusiastic tourist. Porter Ham was my companion on our occasional trips to London, and even a half-century has not dimmed some of the well-etched remembrances. One remains particularly bright in afterimage and loud and clear in echo. It happened on a rather moist Sunday, probably in late June, since we were having a string of unscheduled days after some top-notch thrillers. We had just emerged from witnessing part of a service in Westminster Abbey, and were standing on the wet, shiny paving stones, ears tuned to three contrasting noises. The most regular and insistent, and least readily identifiable, sounded like an unmuffled diesel truck, while other loud but intermittent ones came, considering this was a war zone, from large-caliber guns, and a third sort sounded like clanking chunks of iron from shrapnel falling on the pavement. Glancing up we could see the object of this commotion was a small fast-traveling rudimentary airplane whose trajectory was passing directly over us. It was thrillingly recognizable as a V-1 Buzz Bomb.

"Get in a doorway!" someone yelled, and we did.

At that moment the strange little plane went silent and dumped its nose down into a steep dive. It plunged behind some buildings in the middle distance, emitting an earsplitting blast and seismic shudder, followed by great clouds of black smoke that rose in billowing hemispheres. Of course we ran toward it like small boys, and finally came to a point where we could see the catastrophe. It had struck the St. James Chapel with the Cold Stream Guards and their families at worship, and there were many casualties. We did not approach closely but stood watching the practiced rescue workers do their job. Porter and I had already been to Berlin, but this was our first close view of a real occurrence in the new style total war. It was educational.

Sometimes, back before my combat tour had begun, I would go to watch the return of our B-17s—waiting and squinting at the low sky just above the southeastern horizon even before those in the tower, who would have known by radio, came out on the platform to begin the official watch. It was high drama. There would be red flares arching up from some of the planes as they made their peel-offs, and the waiting ambulances would start for the hardstands of the identified crews. Others would move out when one with a collapsed gear started scraping a seemingly endless scar across the field. I would hold my breath, anticipating an explosion and fire. Death was something that could be expected on a bomb run, but the supreme irony would be to die in the last second of a mission.

We continued our practice, wondering when we'd be added to the real noise of this big machine. Tension was rising. Rumor had it that the invasion could start any day: the beginning of the end—a phrase, as it turned out, too light and insubstantial. Almost a year of bone-grinding, blood-spilling combat lay ahead.

Our early-morning day was coming soon. We'd be posted at 1700 hours the evening before. "Just before the Battle, Mother . . ." I could hear the tune in my head. Did my great-grandfather hum that the night before the first frontal assault on Vicksburg, where he lost his right arm? What did my dad sing? Maybe "Mademoiselle from Armentières" before a mortar shell and mustard gas got him in the Argonne.

Would there be that funny ozone smell in the air? Might familiar voices sound different? The training films didn't give us much to go on, not a very good idea of reality. We only knew reality when something was really happening. We certainly thought about it, though. The sky up there would be dark blue and frost would form in patches on the windows. We would be looking out over the edge of the world very far away. The B-17s would seem still in the air, suspended in a gigantic dome, but the contrails would be racing away behind them at a terrific speed.

While walking back from chow one sunny evening, Porter and I stopped at the PX to buy razor blades and soap, since we still lived in a semi-formal military style, and anyway, beards, no matter how short, were intolerable with the oxygen mask. I also got some Wrigley's Spearmint for high-altitude ear popping and some Milky Ways for my pet kids at Yokehill Farm. I may have started them on their way to tooth decay, but their teeth still looked white enough—coarse food I suppose.

They were neighbor kids by virtue of our unusual proximity and my unmilitary preoccupation with landscape drawing around their place. There were two boys, six and seven, I'd guess—whose only words were, "Any gum, chum?"—and a girl, eight going on nine, who was actually more interested in my drawing, although she didn't refuse the candy bars. The three had a sibling resemblance: all had light-blue eyes with dark pupils, the kind that really looked at you, and they had straight, ill-cut yellow hair, in wind-blown tangles, and rosy country complexions that shone through layers of country dirt. Their clothes were homemade of lightweight material, unnoticeable in color and style. And most likely, as kids, they were invisible to the other guys.

When Porter and I reached the squadron area, Murgatroyd and Pennoyer were standing in front of the posting board. They grinned, giving us the thumbs-up signal, and Pennoyer uttered the famous quip, "You'll be sorry."

It quickened my pulse a little, and I could feel my ears burn.

2

Paris in June
The First Mission

A bothersome light washes over my face, flushing away my dream. It's persistent and vaguely threatening. The light also has an obsequious voice and a respectful hand connected with it. "Sir," the voice says, "time to rise and shine," and the hand gently nudges my shoulder. Rise and shine. What a damn fool expression! And get that flashlight off my face. As I come to the surface, I remember with a slight visceral tightening that I've somehow gotten myself caught up in history's biggest fight, and it's going on right now. The voice says it's 3:00 A.M. We're supposed to be daylight raiders—the Brits do the night stuff—so, what's the big hurry? The Germans are still in the sack. Jesus, it's cold for June. The toilet seat will feel like a stone in the North Sea.

The light moves on, and the patronizing voice whispers again, to someone else, "Sir, it's time."

My nose-bowl comrade, bombardier John Jardine, mumbles something in early-morning nasal. He hacks a little and lights a Camel. The flashlight moves on relentlessly, and our copilot, Porter Ham, gets it next. He says something very quietly in his gentle southern tone, and then our pilot, Russell Lockhart, is respectfully given the message. After that, the light reaches over to Pilot Ken Murgatroyd and his troops at the other end; altogether a strange ceremony, almost a mystic rite.

I sit on my cot for a minute to let the steam slowly rise in my pipes. The visceral disquiet is still there, like a rat in the pantry nibbling, oblivious to outside interference. But anyway, up and at it. I've been sleeping in my long johns, so on with the wool socks, olive drab woolen pants and shirt with official insignias, heavy GI shoes, and that's it. No necktie for the occasion. I had shaved carefully before hitting the sack—the ox mask can be pretty troublesome with a stubble; it can give you the noonday itch something fierce—so I'll see how that works. Maybe we'll not be gone too long; they wouldn't send us to Berlin the first time out.

Jardine is putting on his heavy GI shoes and occasionally blowing his nose. He grunts and sucks in a deep breath and, with his back to me, says, "Hey, Robert, I've been thinking about it; have you considered resigning and going back to Biloxi? Sort of disgraceful, but it'd be good to be a leftover. This stuff is starting to look pretty real."

"Yeah," I say, "but I always refer it to a committee."

"Maybe they'll let you know this evening," he mumbles with a clucking sound.

"How about you, Porter?"

"I like flying," he solemnly answers. "Okay," says John. "It's nice to know that everybody is so ready to do his job; gives me a sense of confidence, and we know that Russell is all business up in that left seat."

We make our visit to the latrine and come out into the dark to wait for the truck. It's 3:15, and it should be getting light, considering it's June and we're at 52 degrees north latitude; but they've screwed nature up a bit with wartime double daylight saving, so it's only really 1:15. The sky is dark, though not black velvet like it can be in our Midwest; but with all the lights off you can see the brighter stars through a slight haze, and there's enough light to see the faces of the other guys. I still have that strange gut feeling I had when I was waiting for the day: I think of Vicksburg and my great-grandad with his mangled right arm and of my dead father with a big flag draped over his coffin and the American Legion firing ear-splitting volleys in the hushed cemetery.

Other crews are gathering across the road—some with glowing cigarettes—waiting for the trucks that are curving up the hill. You can see their squinty little blackout headlights not much brighter than fireflies. I'd like to have walked to the mess hall by myself to think about the enormity of all this, but we're on a schedule, and it's over a mile.

When we get there it's already full of smoke, which gives the yellow walls a greenish tint. It's getting crowded and there's a loud background noise: older boyish voices accented by yelps, much like high school kids before a game. An old proverb says the army makes men out of boys, and today they'll try it on us.

Porter and I sit down together near the steam table and start wolfing our sunny-side-ups. Fresh eggs, and seconds if you're quick, and ham and fried potatoes. We stuff ourselves. It'll be a long hard time until late-afternoon chow.

Porter takes a letter out of his pocket and unfolds it, glances at it, and folds it up again.

"From Marian?" I ask.

"Yup. I'm taking it just in case, you know. Just in case we end up on the sidelines. How come you don't have one waiting, or do you? You've never said."

"I did, but she's pretty strict Catholic, and I'm not much of anything. We might've had a problem, you know. It probably wouldn't have worked out. Our mothers are good friends, and they thought we were okay. But she got involved with a guy from her church club and married him. They'll probably have seven kids, if he makes it through. He's a second louie in the infantry."

We have quick seconds and then some canned pears in red Jell-O. Coffee is consumed with restraint, since we have no wish to expose ourselves at forty below zero up there. We might even do it in our pants the first time a 109 comes at us, but I don't think so.

We ride to briefing over a bumpy road in the same truck. Jardine is dragging deeply on a Camel. He interrupts his conversation with another guy and turns to me, still with his morning nasal, "Okay, Grilley, you're the navigator. Where to?"

"Flak alley, I suppose," is all I can manage. I'm not feeling very clever, but John can always do a job on something funny, and he comes up with a good one.

The brakes squall and the truck stops. We jump out and the driver yells, "Hey guys, lotsa luck." What can I say? Same to you pal? Dawn is starting to show, but the sun isn't up yet, and the air is English damp. A small wave of fear washes up against me again; nothing panicky, only a slightly odd feeling.

A white-legginged MP checks us at the door of the briefing hall. No unauthorized personnel or German spies at this Wagnerian production. It's certainly a theatrical setting, a place where even clichés have deep meaning, my first glimpse of the inner sanctum, and in spite of the nervous levity around me, I'm feeling pretty quiet.

There is a raised platform at the far end of the room with the notorious drape-covered map on the wall above it. We take chairs as close to the front as possible, looking to somehow get the awesome message sooner. Vocal volume increases and the fooling around continues with occasional flippy bits of laughter and graveyard humor. Minutes seem like hours while my eyes follow the wrinkles of the drape looking for a slight tear in it.

After a long few minutes, the door at the far right of the platform opens and our aristocratic-looking colonel strides out onto the platform. Someone yells, "Tenn-hut." With a bumping and scraping of chairs, we jump to our feet, and there is a conspicuous silence following the faint echo. Our commanding officer, Colonel H. W. Bowman, has a surprisingly kind face. He looks like he cares about our fate, though not like a chaplain. Nonetheless he looks as if he expects every man to do his duty, but he's certainly not your stereotyped cigar-chomping Air Force colonel. "At ease, gentlemen. Be seated," he says in a clear voice. I like him, although this is the first time I've seen him.

The draped curtain is pulled back, revealing a very large-scale map of Europe, and there are low-keyed murmurs and sounds of movement. There are no expressions of alarm. Maybe this is a milk run; the experienced guys seem to think so. The thick, bright-red piece of tape runs in an angular roundabout way to Paris. Actually, it runs to Chartres, southwest of the city, then to Melun to the south-east and then back on a heading of about 350 degrees to Le Bourget airfield in northeastern Paris. Coast-out will be at Beachy Head, just east of Brighton.

Colonel Bowman speaks. "This, as you can see gentlemen, is not a long mission, but it's not a milk run either. It's one of considerable importance to the enemy, and to our people in Normandy. German fighter command and major service facilities are located at Le Bour-get, and they constitute a serious threat to our advancing troops. It will be a stoutly defended target, and I wish I could say that you will have complete fighter support. However, there are other forces mak-ing deep runs into Germany, and most of our fighters will be in that area. It's an important target, so give it your best effort."

Next the group intelligence officer, a retread from World War I, gives us a conjectured account of what we might expect in the way of German interference with our plans. He is followed by the weather forecaster who tells us we can expect a clear morning over France and some cloudy patches in the afternoon. There will be very strong northwest winds at our altitude, so we can anticipate a slow bomb run. The chaplain then importunes God to have mercy on us; we sinners, we band of brothers. Actually, I'd like to hear the colonel read Henry V's pep talk to his troops before the Battle of Agincourt.

> This day is call'd the feast of Crispian:
> He that outlives this day, and comes safe home,
> Will stand a' tip-toe when this day is named,
> And rouse him at the name of Crispian,
> He that shall live this day, and see old age,
> Will yearly on the vigil feast his neighbors,
> And say, "To-morrow is Saint Crispian."
> Then will he strip his sleeve and show his scars,

And say, "These wounds I had on Crispin's day."
Old men forget; yet all shall be forgot,
But he'll remember with advantages
What feats he did that day. . . .
. . . .
This story shall the good man teach his son;
And Crispin Crispian shall ne'er go by,
From this day to the ending of the world,
But we in it shall be remembered;
We few, we happy few, we band of brothers;
For he to-day that sheds his blood with me
Shall be my brother; be he ne'er so vile,
This day shall gentle his condition;
And gentlemen in England now-abed,
Shall think themselves accursed they were not here
And hold their manhoods cheap whiles any speaks
That fought with us upon Saint Crispin's day.

(Henry V 4.3.40–97)

I head for the navigators' briefing, and the others to their special preps. I must copy the flight plan as worked out an hour or two ago by the group navigator who no longer flies. It uses the times and required positions specified in the teletyped orders from division. I draw the legs of the flight, coordinate to coordinate, on a blank Mercator chart and on my colored pilotage maps. I'm supposed to fight the war with mathematics: vector lines on Mercator charts and calculations on a circular slide rule called an E6b. At this point, since I will be following a leader, it will be my business to keep an exact account of our position and how we are faring on our timetable. This is called a log, and it is kept with the flight plan on a large ledgerlike form. It also is to include careful notation of the exact time and place of enemy fighter attacks and the location and type of flak encountered, and any observations that may in my judgment be significant. My navigation will consist of a combination of old-fashioned dead reckoning, which is a computation of position made by plotting lines of true heading converted from the magnetic compass reading, with distances measured by true airspeed in combination with wind direction and velocity, and by pilotage, which simply means the visual identification of check points by references to geographical features on the map.

When I leave my special briefing, dawn has become early morning, and a wash of yellow-green covers even the brightest stars in the east. At the distant hardstands, B-17 engines are rumbling in deep dissonance as crew chiefs, who live with their airplanes, are warming them up for our use. I meet my guys outside and go with them to the equipment shop.

An hour and a half after takeoff, or sooner, we'll have ascended to an environment totally unlike that encountered anywhere on the surface of the earth except at the summit of Mount Everest. Our ship is not only unheated and unpressurized but very drafty, and the year-round temperature at 26,000 feet is about forty below zero on either scale, while the atmospheric pressure is about 30 percent of that at sea level. And, of course, there will be a concerted effort by Hitler's followers to kill us sometime today.

These are exciting prospects, and I have to dress specially for the occasion. First, I've started out with a suit of real woolen underwear, which in my former life would have been unthinkable at any time of the year, let alone June. Then, by the rules of military engagement, I wear a basic uniform with my insignia of rank and, of course, dog tags. I also choose to use a "blue-bunny" electrically heated suit, but I'll take my leather sheepskins should there be an electric power interruption. I will wear heavy GI shoes instead of the felt electrics in case I have to spend the winter with the Germans, and large fur-lined boots. An inflatable "Mae West" life preserver is a must, of course, and over that goes a parachute harness with rings on the front to attach a chest pack, should the need arise; but I'll also want to wear a piece of armor called a flak suit, curved segments of steel covered with canvas. Shoulder and underarm snaps holding the front and back together can be released allowing it to drop off so the chute can be attached; clearly a Hobson's choice, since both cannot be worn at the same time. Head covering is also complex, starting

Myself in a flak suit, June 1944. Photograph by Porter Ham.

with a lined leather helmet with built-in intercom earphones. Over that, at about the time the flak suit seems called for, I'll add a large steel pot helmet with hinged dishes covering the earphones down to the jaw level. Also provided, but seldom worn, are thick plastic goggles to protect the eyes from shards of broken Plexiglas and other bits of flying battle debris.

With luck one can manage without some of this equipment some of the time, but no one can do without an oxygen mask in good working condition at altitude. Each person has his mask individually fitted, but to wear it for any length of time is at best uncomfortable and at worst a source of misery. It sometimes seems like a cold clammy hand clutching your face, accumulating breath condensation that often freezes around the edges and sometimes forms ice down in the long flexible tube that plugs into an oxygen-dispensing regulator. This could gradually reduce the supply, so I must squeeze it regularly to break up the ice. In fact, many crewmen in their isolation have quietly died from this hazard; so in order to deal with it, each man is asked to report over the intercom periodically. In addition to supplying my life's breath, the mask contains my microphone, a great improvement over the older throat mike in which clear articulation was lost. I've mentioned that I will be attached to my oxygen regulator, effectively limiting my range of movement, but there will be times however, when greater mobility is necessary. For such purposes we have light-weight "walk around" oxygen bottles that can be repeatedly charged in flight, but their supply is limited to little more than three minutes duration. I will also be tethered by communication wires from my earphones and microphone and by the cord from my heated suit.

I carry some of this stuff by wearing it, some of it in a large canvas bag, and the parachute by its hand-grip straps, and, somehow, my navigator's case. The flak suit is left in the crew chief's tent out at the hardstand; it weighs thirty pounds or more and is too heavy to carry around. After assembling our equipment, we ride again in a truck for more than a mile to the hardstand where our B-17 is waiting. Morning has slipped softly up over a series of low wooded hills to the east and there is a slight mist in the air, but fog is not likely. There's not much conversation. The truck noise seems to preclude it, and I guess that we're entirely inside ourselves.

At the hardstand we throw our things out of the truck and jump down. The big bird, noble and graceful when airborne, looks heavy and earthbound, pregnant with ten 500-pounders. Her gas load has been reduced to 2,400 gallons to accommodate the additional bombs, and Russell and Porter should be able to get her off the ground all right, although in practice we've never lifted this much. The plane is a B-17F without a chin turret, and she is painted a dull olive drab with light-gray undersides. She definitely is middle aged and has been somewhere and back many times; her skin has neat patches in many places and must surely have some major replacements that don't show. There is a wide yellow strip ascending diagonally across her large tail fin with a superimposed black triangle emblazoned with the white letter S, like a medieval war decoration. The crew chief is her resident physician. He has two young assistants who help him deal with her frequently inflicted wounds and her natural ailments induced by the aging process. He assures us that she's in fine fettle, and Russell signs a form indicating that he believes this to be true.

A B-17 is a tail dragger, so its nose is raised, and since it's a large airplane, the hatch on the left underside of the nose is quite a ways up. It's the entryway for those of us who ride up front—bombardier, navigator, pilot, copilot, and top turret, who doubles as flight engineer—and it's expected that young men will easily manage such an inconvenience. I bring my things over from where I've thrown them off the truck and toss them up through the hatch, parts at a time, after which I reach up and grasp the frame on the inside edge of the opening and do a pull-up, climb in and stow my gear in the front, then swing down again.

It will be a little while until the flare ordering us to stations is fired, so we sit by the door of the tent and speculate. The crew chief is a good-natured guy, old enough to be my uncle, and his two assistants are farm boys who cut their teeth fixing tractors and pickups. They are affectionately confident about the old girl and assure us that she has a lot more hours left, and we sincerely try to believe their opinion is justified.

There, arching up in a beautiful parabola, we have our flare, and we clamber to stations. By now the morning sky is quite light, though still slightly green and misty, and the color contrast of the flare looks festive. Another flare and Russell and Porter bring our engines to a low rumble, one through four in order, and we make a very slow sweeping turn out onto the perimeter track and join the long crawl to the threshold of runway two-three. There are about a dozen B-17s ahead of us and perhaps five behind. There is also a like number coming around from the other side of the field, and we are thus engaged for more than twenty minutes. The planes from each line move out onto the runway in turn and are given thirty seconds to run up their engines before the takeoff roll begins, which is long, because at this weight the planes are all ground lovers.

Finally we're in position on the runway, and the low sun at our back makes long purple shadows. The B-17 ahead has lifted off, but it's not climbing very fast and is still outlined against the trees when Russell advances his handful of throttles with the brakes locked. The four Wright Cyclones, pent-up animals, go absolutely wild. They rant and rage at full static thrust, and we are 65,000 throbbing pounds withheld, but straining every ounce in expectation of the miracle of lifting ourselves overloaded into thin air. Glory Bird shakes. She seems to be twitching her tail and everything is moving, yet we're still in the same place.

Suddenly the brakes are released, and the surprised bird makes a promising lurch forward but settles into a slow trundle, and we accelerate like a Mack truck. At first she's got a slight limp, and my guns in their spring suspended mounts swing up and down. The noise is intense, even through my well-padded earphones, and it vibrates in my bones as I sit staring through the bright nose bowl with an occasional glance at the airspeed indicator.

At ninety we're past midpoint; we can't abort. Okay—feeling lighter, beginning to skip a little—there, Russell, a hundred and ten, get her up! Up the gear, Porter—Jesus, we're flying! We howl past three or four stone farm buildings. The chickens must be up by now, as well as their owners; or maybe they've given up and moved away.

A light mist gives atmospheric perspective to the rain-green landscape, and even more than a hundred years later, England is still a Constable painting. The front compartment of a B-17 is certainly a room with a view for which there is no equal, and since we don't use seatbelts, I share the Plexiglas nose bowl with John whenever I have spare moments. My instruments and work table are against the left wall, with generous window space, and my station connections are quite long, so I can easily reach most areas of the compartment, including windows on the other side.

The intense green of the fields seen from low level becomes pastel as we climb. The angular shapes of woods are so clear that they are shown in a deeper color on the detailed pilotage maps, which are in themselves elegant pieces of graphic art.

I give Russell a magnetic heading of 103 degrees, but 100 will do just fine. We are climbing about eight hundred feet a minute at an indicated airspeed of 130, and for the next hour we'll be forming around a radio beacon called a splasher, flying in enormous circles with our radio compasses pointing to a constant 270 degrees. The squadron leads fire marker flares of different colors, so we know who to join in our assigned positions. It's an impressive sight in the bright sunshine, but on a murky day, it'll be a hazardous operation.

Two hours and twelve minutes have passed, and we are at the coast out over Beachy Head, just east of Brighton. The sky is a deeper blue at this altitude, and the sea a softer, grayer hue. The horizon is almost indistinguishable in a luminous mother-of-pearl haze. Geographic features have become maplike, and I can see Hastings, near

Pevensey, where the Normans landed in 1066. I reflect on that. We're still at it—but our ships are going the other way. Testosterone is the fuel that fires these crazy adventures, and there is a new supply with each generation.

The other B-17s seem almost motionless in their third-dimensional echelon formation, but there is occasionally a slight rise and fall as they ride invisible swells. Russell and Porter have their hands full in their turns flying formation at this altitude, since here the ship responds more slowly to yoke and throttles, and the pilot must constantly anticipate her surge or lag. It's a hard day's work. Only the lead planes use their autopilots.

The Channel is sixty-eight miles wide here, so with our tailwind we'll coast in at Saint Valéry-en-Cauxin in about fourteen minutes. It's probably a little fishing village, but only a set of coordinates on my Mercator. When we're at about midpoint, Russell comes on the intercom and asks for an oxygen check and then tells our guys that they can clear their guns, but to take care to not shoot any of our people. They happily comply by blasting off a few rounds; the noise and vibration is rousing.

We coast in at what must be Saint Valéry. Hard to say exactly, since there are a number of villages in that area, but Le Havre and the Seine estuary about thirty miles to the west are sharp and unmistakable. Our ground GIs are slogging away just west of that point and over to the Cotentin Peninsula. This part of France, from our vantage point five miles up, looks happy, or maybe at least normal. War down there is hard to see from up here. Soon we pass a little west of Rouen, where the land is so flat that the wide Seine river has many broad curves and ox-bows. I have a great view, and I'm half convinced that the Germans haven't noticed us yet. I figure our ground speed at 288, so metro wind prediction is just about right on. Jesus, we'll be to Chartres in no time.

At Chartres I'm looking for the cathedral, but I don't have binocs so I just have to use my 20-15 vision. There it is, I think. There's the Chartres Cathedral! The what? The Chartres Cathedral. Christ, I'm talking about art.

The lead box has started a turn to the left, and we in order follow gradually so as not to strain the formation. We're not quite out of the turn, not yet settling on our 78-degree compass heading to Melun, when the top turret guns explode. It's a sudden torrent of noise, almost like having your head bumped. I lurch up against the inertia of my flak suit and half stumble. I've been marking on my Mercator like a school kid and even looking forward to my first free glimpse of Paris, a tourist without a passport gawking while Goering's fighter jocks have been scrambling up into the sun, snarling like the bad guys in *Hell's Angels*. Our top turret has fired a burst prematurely; the bandits are still out of range, though it sure woke me up. But now here they come from twelve o'clock, on a collision course right out of the sun at a 600-mile-an-hour closure. First they're toys with one-inch wing spans, but they grow unbelievably fast, and their guns begin to sparkle. Pyles is hammering again in the top turret, and Jardine is adding to the cacophony. One is coming straight at us. Goddamn, split off you bastard, or you'll get us all killed. He rolls on his back and plunges under us. Null, in the ball, gets a whack at him and Million a split second later in the tail.

Our formation has loosened up in the turn, and the fighters have gone right through it. Anybody hit, or did we hit anybody? With all that lead flying around, somebody must've got it. There's more air than solid substance out there, but somebody's going to be in the wrong spot sometimes.

Here come some more—some more head on again. Holy Jesus. Even through my Ray Bans the sunlight straight from the east is almost unbearably bright. I hunch my shoulders up and hunker my head down like a turtle so the helmet side dishes rest on my flak suit. Jardine has limbered his gun, and Pyles on top is already pounding out his response. It sounds like a bunch of jackhammers on concrete. This 109 coming in also rolls at the last second and swoops beneath us. Null fires again from the ball—just a short burst, but it's such a quick brush that he couldn't have gotten the guy in his sights. The gunners are yelping like beagles, but Lockhart admonishes them to shut up unless they have some news.

Now, the first fighters have come around again, this time from our left at ten o'clock. They're on a pursuiter curve, three rads of deflection. Okay, at least I'm at my gun, but they're past before I can shoot. Damn it. I haven't even charged a round into the chamber. We'd lose if it were for gunners like me. I don't think we got hit, but they must have hit somebody. There's smoke in the lead box.

But now we're turning again. We're at Melun already, and I haven't even figured an ETA, an estimated time of arrival. The lead navigator sure has kept his head out of his butt. How does he do that with all this stuff going on? It was really just academic until Chartres, and there I lost touch. Cope, you have to learn to cope.

The smoking plane in the lead box is really in trouble. I can see orange flame trailing from the left wing. It's falling off to the left in front of us, sweeping out a long descending arc, black smoke painting a wet watercolor brush stroke behind it. If any of them have jumped yet they'd better not pop their chutes until the last minute. With this strong northwest wind they'd land miles further away from our lines.

We roll out on a heading of 352 degrees into a hurricane headwind and settle back to what I calculate to be a ground speed of 172 miles per hour. We have a bomb run of thirty-six miles, and at this pace it'll take about eleven minutes. Now, we're over the southeast suburbs of Paris, but nobody's out in his yard watching us.

And—there's the flak! I was wondering. There's smoke from it up ahead. It's kind of diffused, but there's some in close by the lead box in sharper focus, and it looks like black-velvet popcorn. God, they're giving us the whole damned show today. We don't even have to go to Berlin. Bowman said the Germans would resist, and I guess they are. Jesus, you know, this thing could turn into another Pickett's Charge. They've zeroed in on the lead box, and we're a little lower, so the stuff is going off above us. Pretty soon I can hear some of the falling pieces of shrapnel clattering against us. Time for bomb doors. It's a good thing that Jardine went back and pulled the pins while we had time over the Channel. *Whomp.* They've lowered their fuse altitudes. They're still a little bit high, better high than a bit low, though, because the burst pattern still has some of its upward velocity, but not a whole lot at this upper end of its range. *Bang*—Or actually a very sharp crack. That one, and two more are in so God-awful close that I can feel it in my chest. Glory Bird shudders and plows on, but we sure took something that time. I'm forcing myself to enter position notes on my Mercator, but it's hard to keep my eyes on my paper stuff.

I tell everybody on the intercom that we are about three minutes from bomb release, and Jardine and I have our eyes glued to the bomb bay of the lead plane of our box. I was going to look for the Eiffel Tower, but no way, I guess.

I'm at the nose bowl with Jardine, but now I'm looking down and there it is, Le Bourget, where Lindbergh landed seventeen years ago last month. Our target area is the southwest third of the field where there are many buildings and hangars to be stomped on. I can see flak guns still flashing down on the perimeter. Geez, those guys are pretty brave—or else they think we can't hit the broadside of a barn.

There go the bombs from the box lead, and Jardine hits the salvo switch, crowing, "Bombs away!" We make a 30-degree turn to the left according to the flight plan, and I duly note the exact time of bombs-away, which seems a bit redundant, since every other navigator in the squadron has done the same thing. Our bombs are still falling, but those from the lead box have hit. Null in the ball turret reports great success, but our automatic cameras will tell a more reliable tale. Then about thirty seconds later our bombs hit, and Null says that we stomped them real good.

We continue at our frustratingly slow pace upstream against this huge river of air. This time we'll pass east of Rouen and coast out about ten miles southwest of Dieppe. After passing Rouen, it seems as if we're home free, but near Dieppe several mobile flak batteries take some pot shots at us. Ha! They're not even close, and soon we're out over the Channel, where I get out of my flak suit. A few low fluffy clouds are starting to form under us in the superclear air. From below they must look like the ones in impressionist paintings, Claude Monet clouds. We are down to 18,000 feet and continuing to descend. Coast-in will be at Beachy Head, and I can already see it. I feel a warm relief, almost euphoria, but I keep it in check by remembering that I have thirty-four more of these things to do, and some of them will make this one look like a holiday in the country.

We continue to let down, and at 12,000 I peel off my ox mask. The ice on the edges of it has melted, and it feels wet and slippery. Also, I remember to take off my steel pot helmet, which makes me feel kind of free and easy. John is out of his mask and helmet too with a cigarette alight, and swinging around on his seat he gives me a toothy grin. "Well, Robert," he shouts. "What didja think of that?"

"I'm not going to make it my life's work," I tell him. "But for now it pays pretty good."

"The next one could be the rest of your life's work," he says with what I take for humor.

We're letting down pretty fast now, and the hundreds indicator on my altimeter is unwinding at a good clip. I can clearly see the wave patterns and white caps on the Channel, and Beachy Head is close. My ears have popped several times, and I'm getting really sweaty in this greenhouse, so I start to peel in earnest. We slide under the Claude Monet clouds as I record coast-in, and I catch up a bit on my log, transferring and formalizing some of the scrawls from the Mercator. It's hardly past noon, I note with a twinge of irritation. The Air Force must have inherited Ben Franklin's wisdom from the Army.

The landscape is a very brilliant green, and the bright sun with an absence of haze at our low level renders it in fine detail. These graphic art English pilotage maps even depict churches and country manor houses, and I take a bit of detached pleasure in comparing the symbols with reality.

We swing to the west of London over closely interconnected built-up areas. The towns and cities do not have discrete edges; rather, they reach out along roads and streams to join hands. They have strange or romantic names that must go back to the Middle Ages, and I wonder about their origins. We pass Maidenhead and

High Wycomb, where our high command enjoys its privileges. Next, Leighton Buzzard—what could that name have meant when it was conferred? And, about here we must have crossed a road that Shakespeare used between Stratford-on-Avon and London. And, finally, there's Northampton and the Nene River.

In our turn at last we fly the length of the runway and peel off into a wide 360 to begin our approach. It seems to be kind of an Air Force show thing, a parade review to be filmed for Pathé newsreels, but actually, it's the only organized way to unform a formation. Our final is well judged, and we make a good touchdown on the first quarter, just past the numbers, and decelerate easily with no strain on the brakes. At the hardstand, the crew chief has a smile, and his boys roll their scaffolds up to the engines as soon as the props stop.

I make a rapid calculation that we have been in the air six hours and eighteen minutes, little more than a dress rehearsal for what's to come, but not exactly a milk run; we lost a plane, and some guys may have gotten killed. We ride the truck to interrogation, where, unlike briefing, we are the dispensers of information. As a new crew, we had flown "tail end Charlie" in the low box, and were among the last over the target, the better to see the bomb strike pattern. This all seems redundant, since the film from our automatic strike photo camera was picked up soon after we reached the hardstand, and with it the accuracy can be objectively measured. I give the general position of the fighter attack and a somewhat more precise location of the flak from my log and Mercator, while the severity of this stuff is subjectively attested to by the others. They must take an opinion poll from all the crews, which gives the gravel crunchers something to work with while we rest up. We've been given cake and coffee with Carnation canned milk by a rather good-looking young woman in a Red Cross uniform. I find myself wondering how she spends her off-duty hours near this bastion of high-ranking young heroes. Sounds like stuff for a movie, and I drop the subject.

My log and Mercator are collected for further scrutiny, and my working day is over. A grinning medic, on orders from the flight surgeon's office, gives us each a long shot of Irish whiskey if we wish, and most of us do wish. It's supposed to have a relaxing effect, and it does, particularly since we've had nothing to eat but a piece of cake since breakfast ten hours ago. "Want another?" he asks. "Not at the moment," say I.

At the mess hall the main entrée is a sausage-and-potato casserole, all you can eat, and a choice of fresh brussel sprouts, a canned mixture of peas and corn, or canned carrots—or all if you want. Dessert is thin yellow cake with a hint of white frosting and canned fruit salad, and since coffee is safe now I have two cups, softened by powdered milk and sugar. We really eat pretty well.

Porter and I walk back to the squadron area and find that nothing is posted yet for tomorrow. He says that he's going to write to Marian, and I decide to go to the Landscape. I still haven't sorted things out. I don't care who you are, it's a shocking experience the first time they try to kill you, even if it's all very impersonal and done by guys who might be pretty similar to you. In fact, I'm ethnically half German. My maternal grandmother was born in Potsdam, the daughter of a Prussian soldier, and my father's mother was second-generation German, "Pennsylvania Dutch."

The Monet clouds that were over the Channel have built up into a Constable sky, multileveled and ragged in places. As I walk along the farm path, I can see the cloud shadows move over the barley. There's still a fairly strong wind, and it sends waves through the field, making rhythmic patterns of light and shade. It's only afternoon if you discount the artifice of double-daylight time, but I feel a momentary chill, probably more of an unsettled feeling about the things of the day.

Under the oaks the air seems faintly green compared to the gray clouds, and the last of the hawthorn blossoms still glow pink along the hedges. The hills on a windy day look Romantic, not Classical like they do in still air, and tomorrow I will draw them in the manner of Bonington, if I can. He would have included a woman or a child at a distance—just the right distance, so their proportion would be harmonious with everything else in the picture. If I ever paint a B-17 on approach across the Landscape to runway five, its apparent size must not belie its real size, and it must be exactly placed to create the right scale.

I've reached the end of the lane near the woods and turn back facing the wind. When I pass a tall patch of weeds that has been obstructing my line of sight beyond a bend in the path, I have a broad view, and I can see the cluster of buildings at Yokehill Farm. There is a child coming toward me. Her yellowish hair is blowing forward across her face, and she tries to hold it back from her eyes with her spread-out right hand. She waves with her other hand and begins to run toward me. Her knees and bare feet are a pinkish buff color, slightly darker than the rest of her skin, which, although probably a bit dirty at this time of day, has a glossy appearance and flashes with her running motion.

Lispeth calls out before she's close enough to be understood in the wind. She tries again, and this time I can understand her.

"Did ya go flying today?"

"Yes, to Paris."

"Where's that?" she screams.

"Over that way," I call to her pointing past the east end of the woods.

She runs into me with a squeak and whirls around, sprawling on the grass.

3

Hamburg

Our second mission, flown on June 17, was, in military terms, tacti-cal. We struck a German panzer unit by a process called carpet bombing. They had some surprisingly sharp-tracking 88s; neverthe-less, we didn't get much damage. But three days later, on June 20, we were gotten up at 1:30. Germany, it was Germany, you knew it. Even Lockhart, phlegmatic Russell remarked, "Germany. I guess it's what we came for. The B-26s'll do France." And he kept nodding his head slightly while buttoning up.

"Damn it. I told you this was real," growled Jardine. "They'll send us over there to do something wild. Hey, Robert, what'd your committee say after Paris?"

"Nothing. I forgot to ask."

"Not a thing you can do, but just do it," said Porter, not looking at John but talking to him.

It was really black outside—no stars, a total overcast, though maybe it would break up. We'd had a sunny sunset—English weather, you never knew what to expect. Russell was good on instruments, but could you always trust the other guys? There would probably be a lot of contrails, and forming-up could be tough.

Waiting for the colonel at briefing was something of a flat spot. Porter and I had finished whatever it was we were talking about at breakfast, and we were down pretty much to repetitious speculation, or silence. There was the predictable nervous chatter with an occasional cackle or yip. Several seats away from me a bombardier in the 612th had a fox terrier on his lap. He sat carefully balanced, leaning back in his chair, eyes closed. He stroked the dog's handsome black head slowly, and it seemed to soothe both of them.

"Tenn-hut"—there was Bowman and his coterie.

Everybody jumped. The dog climbed up on the guy's chest, paws on his shoulder, turned its head toward our commander and offered a timid yelp.

"At ease."

Funny thing to say. All he really meant was "Just be quiet. I have something interesting to tell you." The curtain started to move back along its creaking rollers: east further east, past the Netherlands, east along the Frisians—Stop, that's far enough! But it kept right on going to the Schleswig-Holstein peninsula and past. And then it finally stopped. Well, as we all knew it would be, there it was, Germany. HAMBURG in large black letters. Moans, mutterings, and coughs rose to the ceiling. The terrier yelped, and its owner stroked its chest. The red tape left England at Great Yarmouth and angled out over the North Sea at about 50 degrees all the way to the initial point, the IP, Neumünster, in the middle of the big peninsula. Then wham! It turned south and plunged straight down into the lion's mouth.

"As you probably know, gentlemen, Hamburg is not an easy mission, so I'll not try to tell you that it is. However, it's a major oil target, and the enemy will defend it with all he's got." Bowman looked serious, and his entourage nodded their heads in unison, and some shifted to the other foot. "In fact, he regards it as so valuable that he has gone to great lengths to camouflage it. The tanks are underground, and he's built a small imitation suburb over them with streets and houses, and there are some decoy tanks just north of it."

Weather said that clouds would be widely scattered there, but here we'd have a ceiling of 1,500 feet and that we'd be in the clouds to 8,000 or more. Damn, but as I said, Russell was good on instruments—watch out for the other guys though.

Glory Bird was still our old B-17F model, but she had new engines. Russell and Porter both said she was truly an excellent flying machine. Without the twin-gun chin turret she was lighter and more streamlined—got off the ground a little quicker and climbed slightly faster than the newer G models. One gun less was a trade-off that I could accept.

The crew chief and his boys smiled and gave us the thumbs-up blessing as we swung out on the taxiway and began our long crawl to runway two-three. It was still quite dark because of the early hour and heavy overcast. The air was clammy, even a bit foggy, but I didn't sweat the take-off. Russell had Old Bird pretty well figured. In our turn, the Wright Cyclones howled, full blown at forty-eight inches, and we trundled first slowly; at midpoint, feeling lighter, we began to rush. Two-three was easily the longest runway, and a relatively smooth one. We were off with plenty to spare, but the green landscape was missing. In place of it, dark-gray silhouettes stood flat against an indefinable background. But not for long. We entered the muffy lower edge of the clouds at about 1,200 feet more or less, where their translucence was soon blotted out and they took on the color of wet concrete. At irregular intervals we shuddered through brisk rotational turbulence, the vortex pattern from an invisible plane ahead. At 9,000 feet shafts of light began to poke through dips in the cloud tops. Then early sunlight and intensely white contrails twirled in a dizzying mix through dark-blue sky, and arching colored flares painted messages in and out of sight. Airplane parts—tails, wings, and engine nacelles—flashed by sometimes closer than intended. The ADF radio compass needle crawled around to its correct 270 degrees as we drew broad circles around the splasher. Some order out of chaos was happening, and the formation was up and running with no catastrophes—a dazzling and, at times, frightening procedure.

About thirty miles north of the Dutch Frisians, the undercast began to break up, and the deep ultramarine North Sea fanned out ahead to an indistinct shell-gray horizon. As in my premission vision, the B-17s rode smooth as ships on a quiet ocean, their slight period of undulation in relation to each other was the only noticeable movement. An equivocal illusion made them seem to be suspended by invisible wires from an immense dome. My real perception of space was more voluminous than it's possible to describe. Reality can only be understood by experience.

They hadn't, as yet, given me a Gee set, so my navigation was still based on air plot and pilotage, but I had our position quite accurately. We were making a ground speed of about 240, and in twenty minutes we were passing the island of Helgoland, which was known to have a fighter base where, I'd heard, they used twin-engine JU-88s as night fighters to attack the Brits. We saw none, and in another ten minutes we were crossing the Schleswig coast at a little place called Meldorf, a fishing village, I'd guess, and then on to our IP at Neumünster.

"Okay guys," Russell warned, "if you don't have your flak suits on now, you better snuggle into them, we're getting to where we're going."

And there they came—right out of 12 o'clock high, fighters straight out of the sun, like at Chartres. Pyles was blasting away, and again it was like a jackhammer on pavement. Then Jardine managed a couple of shots, and an FW-190 plunged inverted under us with Null roaring from the ball and then Million from the tail. Another and another—there was some ragged metal tearing up from the left wing tip but no fire—and then they came around from 10 o'clock, standard modus operandi. This time I at least had charged my gun—there, three rads and fire in bursts—I did, way out there at all that air. I never saw one go through my sight rings, but I used three rads lag—Jesus I tried. There were shell casings rolling and clattering around on the floor, and I nearly fell down on some, and to think we were just getting started. Somebody on the right side of our element was dropping back. He had two props feathered with smoke but no fire. I didn't know who it was; Lockhart had the formation diagram flimsies.

Ten miles short of Neumünster we started a slow turn south. I could see the big Elbe estuary off to the right, clear as the map—and just like Jardine said—this stuff was getting real. When we were all the way through our turn and heading straight south to the target fewer than forty miles away, I could see wisps of black smoke rising from it in irregular puffs and growing.

Then, in five minutes we were getting into heavy flak and it looked worse than the pictures of box barrages we'd seen. They didn't shoot at us individually; they just filled the sky up with shrapnel so there were very few holes that you could get through. They had a thousand guns, and each one kept shooting shells up into the same spot and there it was for miles out in front between us and the target, a giant cluster of invisible points that opened up like bushels of black-velvet popcorn. We were flying between the bursts at varying distances. The closer ones were large curling shapes that seemed to be passing rearward at high speed, making harsh noises—something between a jarring bump and a sharp crack that I could feel as well as hear—and raking us with shrapnel, tearing holes of differing sizes in planes and people. God, what a mess.

Old Bird was being savaged. Our room with a view took shrapnel right and left. One piece tore through my desk and would have hit me in the face, but I was standing half-turned, and it struck the back of my flak suit. It felt like a hammer blow, and I instantly reached to probe the spot. There was no blood on my glove, no wound. The canvas cover over the steel was torn. I was impressed; this was a good piece of work clothes, the best suit I'd ever had.

It was happening all through the ship. Our gas tanks were hit many times, but the pieces were small and the self-sealing liners held. It was getting pretty drafty, though, and at forty below, I tried to cover every bit of my face, yet ice formed on the edges of the mask like a frozen hand.

God, there went one in the lead box. *Wham,* and fire all over. The expanding nova just missed the plane to its left as it fell, but not by much. We were about two minutes to release, a long two min-utes. I never knew that two minutes could be so long. We got into somebody's prop wash for a moment, and Glory Bird hopped around a bit, but Russ got her back steady in time for the drop. The target was starting to burn heavily from the strikes of the group ahead of us. Certainly the little camouflaged suburb was a waste of plywood or whatever they used to build it."

Bombs away," yelled Jardine in his husky voice, and we started a long slow turn to the right. The flak was there waiting, still a barrage, and we moved on through it.

We lost another plane to flak-bite while we were still in the turn, but this one didn't blow up; it just slipped away in a slow burn. There were some chutes—maybe they all got away, maybe. After we'd gotten out of range of the flak, damn, if there weren't some more fighters. They came after us from about eight o'clock, like a sheriff's posse—Jesus, this was a long working day, and it wasn't even noon.

They made two passes, neither directly at Old Bird, and were gone, probably on their way to dog the group behind us. I couldn't tell if they hit anybody in our outfit, but we didn't need any more reminders to go home. Lockhart called for an all-positions report and found that we still had a full crew, nobody even hurt.

We angled coast-out north of Bremerhaven and got some tracking flak from one of the Frisian Islands, pretty mild stuff though. The dark-blue North Sea looked really cold, but I was glad to see it, because at that point it seemed like we were going to get home. Pyles reported that we'd not actually lost much fuel, considering the blasting we'd taken. I carefully transferred the chicken scratching from the working Mercator to my log. The interrogation officer, like a grade school teacher, praised the neatness of my first two logs but didn't pay much attention to the Mercators. They only kept them from the lead.

I got out of my flak suit and took a look at the damaged part. It had been ripped badly. I was curiously happy for a moment, and then sad—damn it, there were thirty-two more of these things waiting to ambush us, and like Jardine kept saying over and over again, "It's pretty real."

When we got back to Deenethorpe the clouds were well dissipated, so after all that pounding we at least didn't have to sweat one of those groping around in the weather letdowns. The meat wagons were busy, though. There were enough wounded to keep the doctors and nurses busy for the rest of the afternoon, and I don't know how many went to the morgue. The crew chief was quite unhappy when he got a good look at Old Bird—she was not going to fly again very soon.

Interrogation dragged out for the better part of an hour, even for us greenhorns, but what the hell, redundancy was the way those guys made a living. My rear end was tired from sitting on the food crates they used for chairs, and I was glad to see the flight surgeon's man with the Irish. I took two, and somebody, maybe Porter, gave me his second.

The mess officer must have tried to do his best. We had ham stew with plenty of meat. Naturally the vegetables in it were canned, but I guess the Brits grew barely enough for themselves, so who could complain? I had white cake and two cups of coffee and still had a little buzz from my three shots. Next time two would be plenty, even if I felt pretty wound up. I didn't want to get sick in front of anybody—a bad show, and I was still somewhat status conscious.

Porter and I walked back. It had turned into a warm, sunny afternoon, and exercise was good after the hours of static tension and muscle-numbing fatigue. Although I had a seat in the room with a view, I had spent hours on my feet with more than fifty pounds draped over me; and the other guys, each in his own form of torture, came back exhausted.

Porter and I were both convinced that we'd be sent back to Germany the next day—it looked like good weather, and General Jim and the other old men at High Wycomb were on a roll—new B-17s coming in and new crews, together with lots of bits and pieces. They were flush. And I wouldn't be surprised if the ghost of Grant was poking at them—"Sock it to 'em. You don't win wars letting your

men sit around on their butts." Porter thought Lee was a real gentleman but that he'd spent his men pretty extravagantly.

At 1700 hours we were posted for the next day, and I again
wished that I hadn't had those three long shots. I didn't feel sick, just
tired. Maybe a walk in the Landscape would be the thing so I could
sleep later on—at five o'clock double-daylight it was just the middle
of the afternoon, time for a walk.

I was lying on the grass somewhere in the Landscape with my eyes
closed; must have been in the shade, out of the brightness, where I
could feel the soft damp green of the grass and a faint breeze on my
face. I guess I was asleep, or certainly unwound, dreaming maybe, or
about to. A fly touched my nose just lightly, and I brushed it away
with the back of my hand. There it was again on one of my eyelids. I
brushed at it, but it was more like a spider web or maybe a very thin
stalk of grass, this time on my cheek. I blinked and opened my eyes
to a squint. It was Lispeth, my grimy little Bouguereau, her face tilted
slightly to one side with a calm expression, as if she had been pa-
tiently waiting a long time for me to wake up. When she saw that I'd
risen to the bait, she erupted with a bubbling giggle and raised her
hands above her forehead, palms a few inches apart and spread her
fingers, curling them backward. She ended her laugh abruptly and
brought her fingertips down to my cheekbones pressing ever so
lightly. It was a strange but quite original little gesture.

Next Freddy, whom I'd not noticed at first, thrust his pink and
greenish baby satyr's face over her shoulder, grinning and presenting
his cupped hand. "Any gum, Chum?"

4

Landscapes and Elizabeth

Before Paris, I'd regarded my discretionary time as something lightly given, a happy turn of circumstances soon to be taken away, so what actually materialized could hardly have been imagined. Summer was certainly the time to make war when one might be expected to keep at it until he finished his tour, or got knocked down; but there it was, plein air drawing in an exotic landscape, hour after hour, with room and board thrown in for good measure, and even a chance to replenish my supply of handmade paper from Winsor & Newton in London.

Such a pursuit must have placed me in a minority of one in the entire Eighth. One couldn't be absolutely sure, but it seemed like a good bet. Creativity and self-expression were, of course, rampant. Inspired amateur figure painters from the sign shops spent many happy hours doing "nose art" to slightly titillate the common taste, and there were poets, the serious ones, and limerick makers, the latter of whom I favored, and journal keepers by the hundreds, a source for future historians. And then, too, there were unauthorized photographers like my friend Porter, to whom I'm indebted for the portrait of me in my flak suit, helmet, and ox mask. They were all moved in one way or another by the human necessity to leave their mark and tell the world what had happened.

My drawing, though, was totally self-centered, a student study abroad, the harbinger of what I was going to do with my life after "the duration-plus." So you could say landscapes and Elizabeth were preordained, all part of my graduate work.

My first glimpse of the children came during a session of drawing farm buildings, when I glanced suddenly in the direction of a wagon standing in the lane and saw their three faces pull back behind it. They did not reappear, so it didn't turn out to be a meeting, though I did half expect an adult to step outside and question my intrusion, so a courteous request for permission next time might be in order, admitting to being the unlikely combination of artist and bomber navigator.

The next day I came with an offering of Milky Way bars, and you could suppose they smelled them, so quick did they come out of hiding. I held out my hand, asking, "Gum, chum?" and thought it would be an easy transaction, instant friendship.

Not so fast, the girl seemed to say, and she raised her arm to restrain the boys. They stood motionless for a moment squinting at me in the bright sun, and when she sensed they were about to dash forward anyway to claim their due, she lowered her hand, and in ten seconds they were tearing the wrappers off.

She watched them without expression until the older one was nearly finished, then turned back to face me and began to walk at a measured pace, as dignified as a barefoot kid ever gets. She stopped within three feet of me and I presented the candy. Instead of reaching for it, or even looking at it, she stared at the drawing and back at my eyes. Her brow was slightly furrowed, and her upper lip was raised in the center enough to show two relatively new teeth, one slightly misaligned. We faced each other for another ten seconds, and she accepted the Milky Way, dropping it into the depths of her skirt pocket seemingly without interest. Then she shifted her weight to her right foot and extended the left one forward at a toe-out angle, with a slight bend of the knee. Contrapposto! How did she come by that? It's conventional posture for classical sculpture, but

53

kids, in confrontation, normally stand knees locked back. She even relaxed her right shoulder and tilted her head, perfecting the balance. Exceptional; it was as if she'd been coached. But still her sandy-colored eyebrows were tilted up toward the center of her forehead, and her lips were parted. Either she was a mouth breather or she wanted to say something but couldn't quite get it out. Plainly she was waiting, and I realized what it was.

"You want to see it?" I asked

She nodded two or three times. Her whole face relaxed, almost smiled, and she drifted around to my left elbow, looked at the drawing and at what it represented, then back at the drawing. She drew a long breath and curled the tip of her tongue against her upper lip.

"That's good."

She paused and half closed her eyes. "You an artust?"

"Going to be," I said, "when the war's over."

"But yer a soldier now?"

"Yes, I'm a flying soldier."

A perfectly round cloud covered the sun, and the furrow was there again on her forehead.

"Will ya get killed then?" she asked.

"Of course not," I answered.

She looked toward the squadron area and was silent.

"Can I ask your names?" I asked.

She turned back toward me with a not entirely cheerful face. "I'm Lispeth, and they're Winston and Freddy."

After the boys finished their Milky Ways and saw there were no more to give, they lost interest and ran up the hill where they began to throw sticks into a tree. I couldn't tell which one was which.

"Lispeth, do you think you should go in and ask your mom if it's all right for me to be out here drawing?"

She nodded her head, flicked the hair out of her eyes, and resumed her contrapposto stance. "Oh, it's okay. She knows yer out here and says it is—that yer a flier from Deenethorpe, not a tramp."

I was pleased, and thought it was a nice thing for the mom to say.

My drawings still lacked something. There were the usual mistakes of drawing what I expected to see instead of what I saw. They were smooth, without character, but, anyway, recognizing the problem was a first step. I stood up from the weathered wooden box I'd been sitting on, stretched, and set to work again. It was unusually quiet. The boys had stopped throwing sticks in the tree and gone off somewhere. Lispeth sat cross-legged a little ways away to watch, and from time to time she came over to judge the progress, also to assure me that it was awfully good.

The kids, as I've said, had light yellow hair. Their eyes were light blue, with specks of amber that caught the light on sunny days. They seemed to be of quite healthy build, considering the national food limitations. You could assume that farm people fared better than city dwellers, so there were extra benefits for children sent up from London and the other bombing targets. Kettering had an enlarged population of kids, and there were some living in the village of Upper Benifield. How the school problem was managed, I have no idea. Lispeth was not going to school in May when I first intruded in the Landscape.

I continued to pay my toll in candy and gum. The boys grinned and took it hopping up and down, then bounded away squealing, "Gum, chum." Lispeth would take the treat with tongue pressed against her upper lip. Sometimes she'd smile briefly and even giggle.

After about a week I began to work more on tree and field landscapes in the pasture west of the farm buildings. It had fine hill curves with tall cumulus clouds that would build by afternoon, Classical; Poussin or Claude, almost Elysian. My drawings began to improve, and sometimes I used iron-oxide chalk pencils on warm gray handmade paper, giving them a museum tone that pleased my anachronistic soul.

It was almost the first of June, and still the wedge of time continued to hold. I had been to London once, but there was an increasing tension after we were, for unexplained reasons, told to carry our .45 automatic side arms. I was pretty sure that something would happen soon and soldiering business would interrupt my studies.

Lispeth started to follow me around to watch. Certainly she had never seen drawings except those done by children, and she was fascinated. I decided to make some of her, and she was pleased. One might suppose she wondered what it would be like to see her image on paper. It would be a waste not to use her as a model. Having grown used to me, there'd be no self-conscious unease, and she was naturally graceful—a nice tilt to the head. She might have had a pretty quality about her if she were in the care of a well-to-do city family. As it was, she had a ring of dirt around her neck and a runny nose, and her hair looked to be haphazardly cut, but it wouldn't have mattered in a drawing. Botticelli could have done a job with her, and Andrea Del Sarto's models may well have been smudgy.

I tried to guide her into her first standing pose, which was nonsense, carrying coals to Newcastle. She needed only to be told to stand still—arms in optional positions—and she had more patience than I would have expected. Even her usually grave expression gave a certain elegance to the pose.

I made several more drawings of her before the sand in the hourglass ran out, and my ability to draw was redirected to navigator's airplots. Lispeth was delighted by her unexpected specialness. Often she looked at her slender arms and hands, rotating them through graceful angles, and I could imagine her using the household's mirror to see how they looked to me.

I didn't come back to draw in the Landscape until after Paris, when I'd become a shot-at veteran, no longer concerned about borrowing time from General Jim. Lispeth saw me from a distance and ran very fast with the strong wind blowing her hair across her face. She kept brushing it back with her right hand and waving with the other.

One day, after a less-than-spectacular combat trip, as I sat, my back to the Oak, reading Stephen Crane's *The Red Badge of Courage,* I was distracted by the kids engaged in a minor row. With mild curiosity, I looked up to watch and saw Lispeth sprinting up the hill in pursuit of Freddy. He'd gotten a head start but of little advantage, since she ran over him with the ease of a cheetah. Then she kept him down by adroit kicks and shoves of her right foot, hollering louder than I'd supposed she could, "Get outta here and leave me alone!"

Then she allowed him to escape by sidling crab-fashion and running a few steps backward, yelling insults that I couldn't translate but that certainly must have been small-fry obscenities.

Of course, she went after him again, and with some remarkable hound-and-hare maneuvering ran him to ground in a fast turn, where she lost her own balance and fell over him. After a five-second struggle, she planted her knees on his squirming shoulders and gave him the feel of her sweet little knuckles just above his left ear. She continued to kneel on him for a while longer, but when his strainings had lost their steam, she mockingly patted him on the cheek and climbed off.

For a few seconds she stood hands on hips watching his retreat. Then she turned toward me with a warmth of satisfaction in her cheeks and, after a pause for emphasis, came over for a visit. Sitting down with none of the inhibitions of a well-brought-up little girl, she looked me in the eye, allowing her expression, whatever it meant, to become a smile that asked, "How did you like that?"

When she noticed the book closed across my thumb, she half-hopped and slid around beside me and sounded out the title, *The Red Badge of Courage*, pronounced slowly in her exotic dialect. "What does it mean?" she demanded. "Read it to me."

"Lispeth, honey, it's a grown-up's book and kinda sad. You wouldn't like it."

"Yes I would. Read it," she moaned, making little agitated up-and-down motions with her shoulders and elbows that progressed to her hands. She continued with slight huffing and whining sounds, indicating she was not going to be put off.

"No," I said, closing the book. "Forget it."

5

Berlin

June 21, the day after Hamburg—it came sooner than I'd expected—
a 1:30 thing again, and that corporal with the fatigues and floppy hat
was in with his flashlight and dulcet words. I was closest to the door
so I always got it first.

Jardine woke up with a partially controlled eruption of coughing
and cursing. He lit a cigarette as fast as a frog tongues a fly and cried
out in full husk, "Does this mean war?"

By that time Lockhart and Ham were awake.

"Hey, John, didn't anyone ever tell you not to volunteer?" asked
Russell.

"Aw, Christsake, Lockhart, I never volunteered," he groaned.
"You know I never volunteered—always advised against it. I was just
sitting in a bar one night minding my own business, and a buncha
MPs came in, subdued me, and hauled me away. Next thing I knew,
I was flying."

"Well, can you beat that?" asked Porter. "I always thought that
you volunteered because you're so patriotic."

"Yeah, you bet he is," said Russell. "He'll have to sit there right in
the middle of our bay window and be a bullseye for those 109 jocks."

Well, that was sure different than yesterday morning—either it
was so early we were still drunk, or maybe it lightened up a little

when you made it back from a few of these. After that bit of levity, things settled down. Germany was still the obvious guess. A far-away place in Germany, judging by the time. Everyone was quiet, buttoning up and putting on shoes. Death was still out there waiting somewhere.

The sky was black again. A carbon of yesterday, and the fooling around was not repeated in the truck while we banged down the gravel path and road to the chow hall. I didn't feel very hungry, so I had to stuff it in. You'd die on your feet if you didn't, but you could die on your feet even with a full stomach in this line of work.

The bombardier had his fox terrier at briefing again—said its name was Jimmy—no disrespect intended to the general, simply a coincidence. His crew chief doggy-sat for him while he was away on business. A traveling man should always have someone to come home to. He said he was going to leave everything to Jimmy in his will so he'd be well taken care of in his old age. Man's best friend, you know. Dogs fight sometimes, but anyway, they almost never kill each other, that is, almost never. And just look at us; we try to do it every time.

The guy had a philosophy there, I had to agree.

"Tenn-hut."

Everybody leaped, and the dog barked—all a matter of respect. I still thought Bowman had a nice face and was quite liberal with our social liberties, but I was getting a little tired of him at this time of morning. Maybe I was in the wrong business. I was usually tired this time of morning, especially the second day in a row, so I almost fell on my chair when he gave us at-ease.

The curtain rolled back slowly, to heighten the suspense—back past Hamburg. There were cries of alarm. The guy with the dog had his hand clamped over its muzzle, but still it managed a yelp.

Jesus, it was Berlin, a punishment raid.

Since our Old Bird had been plucked, and on the back shelf for a while, we got a B-17G, not a new one though. It still had an olive drab and gray paint job, but it was equipped, as the model letter indicated, with a double–gun power chin-turret, and for me it had an electronic line of position indicator called Gee. It was like getting a magic set for Christmas. I was now master of latitude and longitude, at least over England, the North Sea and the Lowlands. I could even use lines of position to guide Russell in on an instrument letdown. I knew how to use it all right—part of the practice we'd been doing in May.

The weather was the same as it had been the day before but with more extensive cloud cover over the North Sea and the northwestern part of Europe. Berlin would be clear though, lucky Berlin.

We took off at 0442 hours and had the same exciting time while forming. The contrails were worse, and the whole thing seemed like an abstract painting. Two ships brushed wings and had to stagger down through the mop-colored clouds while two standbys had to come chasing after us. They didn't catch up until we reached the wing buncher at Glatton, and they had to push to do it.

The North Sea lay hidden under a smooth white cloud sheet all the way, and I took at least twenty Gee fixes; more to practice than for need, since I was not at that point a lead navigator. We coasted in at Meldorf and had a brief but sharp fighter attack about the time we reached Neumünster. Our squadron was not hit, but a B-17 from the 615th began to drop back with a feathered prop. I saw no smoke from it and could only hope that those aboard made it back without ditching in the cold North Sea, which, even with life rafts, could take your breath away forever.

From about seventy miles or more north-northwest of Hamburg, two very large columns of black smoke from our target of the day before could be seen rising through the cloud cover—marvelous—I was filled with shameless joy. Maybe it would shorten the war by at least several days.

After reaching a body of water called Schaal Lake, we passed the edge of the cloud layer about 130 miles northwest of Berlin—this was a fighter place, and every eye was straining for black specks that could suddenly grow into devils. But in truth German fighters, the hunters, were also the hunted. P-51 Mustangs were more than a match for them and could now, with special drop tanks and other equipment, make it this far. It was not really accurate to call them escorts, since they did not in fact fly along with us; their real mission was to seek and destroy the enemy, often right over their home bases. The escort system, as it was conceived, involved a coded call for help if we were under determined attack, but it worked more by chance than with certainty. Many groups came and went without fighter intervention, but the overall power of the Mustangs was clearly beginning to show, particularly at the hot spots, like Berlin. For instance, northeast of Brandenberg that day we saw 51s in a display of aerobatic frivolity, if you can accept that paradox, and it brightened our pathway awhile.

We reached our IP at Zehdenick about fifty miles north of Berlin at 0956 hours and tightened up for the twelve-minute bomb run. We would use a releasing device called an intervalometer, which evenly spaced our eight 500 pounders to do the most extensive damage. By that time our group was entering a very dense barrage, and my teeth were clenched and eyes squinting. Jesus, what a way to make a living. It was like Russian roulette.

And there was Berlin, already deeply disordered by the RAF under moonlight. In bright sunshine it looked like a great gray mass. Streets were by then blurred by fallen stone and bricks, and yet there was more for us to do. What had they done about the Kaiser Frederick Museum and its magnificent collection? And the great historic monuments? The lofty columns with bronze chariots? The architects had built for centuries then the crazies took over and made things like this happen.

John yelled bombs-away at 1006 hours, and we turned sharply to the west and then to the northwest. There was a momentary respite from the flak, and then it began again in full fury. There were two smokers from the lead box and two from our own. We were taking quite a bit of dense smoke from one of ours, and it was pouring into our ox regulators until it began to drift off to the left and Russell squeezed a bit more to the right. Chutes appeared, and the plane began to angle down with orange flames starting to show. Our other one hung right in there, and soon the smoke stopped, but his number-three engine was feathered. Then he began to settle out of the formation, to where the sharks would glean him up. By 1058 we were back up to Neumünster heading for the North Sea without further fighter strikes. We had flak damage, but it didn't seem as severe as that from Hamburg, at least not in the nose section. Lockhart called for an all-positions report, and it seemed to be the case throughout the ship. But we weren't home yet—yesterday fighters hit us at this same spot. We'd come back over the cloud sheet before reaching Neumünster and were not to see the North Sea again on the way home, but we got no tracking flak or sporadic fighter passes.

Once past Helgoland we started a long gradual letdown, but except for my flak suit, I was not in haste to get undressed. Jardine had his flak suit and helmet off early as usual, and when we were down to 22,500 feet he pulled off his oxygen mask and lit a cigarette. He swiveled around with a broad grin and said something to me that I couldn't understand because he didn't say it through his mike. Dragging deeply on his Camel, he stood up and strode back to the space under the flight deck, where he appeared to say something to Porter. Suddenly he sagged to his knees and leaned heavily against the door frame for a moment on his way to the floor in front of me. I clamped his mask back on and gave him a jolt of pure oxygen.

"What the hell are you doing, John?" I asked as he blinked and shook his head.

"For Christsake," he mumbled. "I'll have to quit drinking and smoking and get back in shape—can't even stand 12,000 feet anymore.

"You sure missed that one. It's 22,000 feet; you didn't see the little white needle, and you're a bombardier."

At a point about 150 miles closer to home, we were down to 12,000 feet and I took off my steel pot and ox mask. I kidded him about it, but Jardine made no further mention of his peculiar mistake.

We coasted in at Cromer at 1245 hours down to 4,000 feet but still over clouds, about an eight-tenths covering, and at 1308 took a radio compass reading heading for Deenethorpe. In about twenty minutes we were on landing line of position with help from my new toy Gee box. The clouds were broken at six-tenths, and we touched down at 1326 after eight hours and forty-four minutes in the air.

Our battle damage was definitely not as bad as it had been at Hamburg. The crew chief who had inherited the Bird was relieved—it only needed some nighttime sheet-metal work and a new prop blade.

After interrogation, I took no more that one shot of Irish. I was relaxed enough just to get home, and though I was pretty tired, chow tasted good and I ate quite a bit.

Again at 1700 hours we were posted for the next day. At this rate we'd be buying property in Germany soon, or be sent home in a box. Even Porter was starting to swear. He went in to write Marian—maybe his last chance. I was too tired to write to my mother.

I walked for a while in the Landscape and was glad that I'd had only one shot of Irish. When you were tired it made you feel even more so—not just relaxed. Must be to France tomorrow though, not to Germany.

After a while I sat down on the grass in what would have been the shade if it had been sunny. The broken clouds showed some blue, but the breeze was cooler than it had been for several days. I leaned my elbow on the ground and picked two or three yellow wildflowers from a patch that I had happened into.

Liz didn't surprise me this time. When she saw that I'd noticed her, she raised her hand as high as her chin and waved with her fingers. She was barefoot and bare armed from the shoulders but wore a little unbuttoned vest sweater. The cool English summers bothered these kids not at all.

When she was within three feet of me, she dropped to a cross-legged sitting position and looked at me with a noncommittal expression somewhat short of a smile. The breeze rustled her uncombed hair, and she flipped at it with her mobile fingers.

"You haven't made a draw'n a me in a lon while," she said in an unmodulated voice. "You used to drawr the trees a lot, an me. My

Mum likes the draw'n a me you gave us. Said you must be a very good artust." She raised her head slightly, tipping her forehead back and her chin foreword a little. "I'd like ta drawr too. You think I could?" With that question she allowed her lips to remain open as if to add another word, but none came, and I could see her slightly misaligned upper left front tooth.

Memory plays fast and loose with its talking pictures. There are images that you cannot for sure attribute to remembrance, and there are those that may well be informed inventions that blend seamlessly with recall. I'm quite sure that she had a misaligned upper left front tooth, but I cannot with certainty remember the spelling of her family name. Voices are even more elusive, and while the gist of what might have been said a week earlier can have substance, a transcript, if you wish, would not be likely.

I know that Elizabeth spoke pre-wireless Midland country dialect, clipping certain syllables unexpectedly, making another language out of our versatile English; this with a child's high, sweet inflection. It seems that I can hear the sound of it, almost, but maybe I hear her re-creation on a Masterpiece Theater period production; yet how would they know for sure what it sounded like? Somebody would have to remember, or maybe it can still be found if you go far enough out in the country.

"Yes, I'll get you pencils and paper, even colored ones."

She looked pleased. "When?"

"Next time I go to Kettering." I could tell that now would have been a better answer, so I said that she could use some of mine until then.

6

Frevent

June 22. Number five came the next day, the third day in a row, but the wake-up call was flashed at 3:30, a kindness of sorts. Maybe it was just back to Paris, a scenic trip up the Seine. I won't quote Jardine, but his comments could easily be imagined—actually I enjoyed them—they improved my mood. Nevertheless, we had to be careful not to let ourselves get too cheery; you could get killed at the Pas de Calais with one potshot, so John's points should certainly have been given some credence. Russell even suggested that we might consider ourselves lucky—after all, back in the old days people our ages died of natural causes right and left.

Our friendly wake-up agent came back a few minutes later and said that the major had reason to think that we could dress lighter because, while he couldn't be specific about it, we weren't going to go so high—so high, what did he mean "so high"? I decided to take my sheepskin anyway—sometimes I even got cold on the ground on a cloudy day, and the summer's warmth had fallen far short of spring's extravagant promise.

At breakfast, and while waiting for briefing, I was kidded a lot about my fragility. Some suggested that maybe I should apply for a transfer to the South Pacific, and there were those who wondered if I really was from Wisconsin. Still, I was satisfied with my choice of garment. I could sweat more comfortably than freeze. Up to that point rumor had pronounced today's trip a milk run, but in my view, and I shared this with John, there was no such thing. Certainly it wouldn't be another Hamburg or Berlin, but the fighting in Normandy remained pretty hot and heavy, and the Germans still had their shooting irons warmed up.

The colonel, good officer that he was, did not say anything that would support the notion that it would be a milk run. He simply said that our target, a large number of camouflaged tanks and self-propelled guns hidden near a village called Frevent, would be hard to spot and that we would be going in at 14,000 feet in the hopes of attaining greater accuracy.

The Germans did have some unexpected 88s limbered up about fifty miles short of the target, and at 14,000 feet we were naked, so up we went. I certainly didn't know that loaded B-17s could climb that fast, but we were up to 22,000 feet in a hurry. In spite of this change in plan, our circular error was fairly good, according to the strike photos, and we lucked out as to casualties—no one killed, but two or three wounded, though there were a lot of chilly personnel.

We got back to Deenethorpe well before noon; hardly a day's work for a day's pay, but with Paris, Hamburg, and Berlin among our first five, our employers were well ahead of us.

It was a partly sunny day, and I wasn't at all tired, having sacked-in until three-thirty, so after chow I rode my bike into Kettering to browse in the used-book store. Sometimes I found some unexpected things, I should say, usually I did, and they were cheap because of our comparatively high pay. That time I found two small inexpensively bound books, a matched pair, that intrigued me—*A Hundred Hands* and *A Hundred Feet*. They were reproductions on yellowish paper of details of hands and feet from old master drawings. At two shillings a piece, you bet. I also bought a ragged copy of Oscar Wilde's weird little guilt trip called *A Picture of Dorian Gray* and a small well-preserved *Poems of Keats*—why would anyone sell it?

The next day it rained hard all day, and there was no mission—none had been posted—and the turnout at breakfast was light. I ate cookies and read Oscar Wilde—rather light stuff for such a famous writer. But by real chow time I was hungry, and having proven my prudence with the purchase of a big black English umbrella, I arrived at the mess hall wet only below the knees.

Still there was no mission posted for the day after and it turned out to be clear, even rather warm. The Landscape was my choice—I was beginning to do things worth keeping. Both my technical skill and ideas about how to use it were well on their way, and someday when everybody's anger had settled down, I would be an artist, my uncle's prophecy that I couldn't make a living at it notwithstanding.

But since he was, by and large, a kind and generous man, he would criticize in terms meant to inform rather than hurt. For example, my mother, as anyone could see, did not profit from her two years at Chicago's Art Institute. But he allowed that she had earned her own support, so no one could complain, because in a way she did improve her mind and, after that fling, was able to get down to business and use her college training as a school teacher in the country, first through eighth grade. I, he advised, should study engineering, since I was a bright kid and good at making things.

But precisely because I was good at making things, I came easily to problem solving in making realistic images—drawings. My uncle admitted that that was clearly so, but this talent would surely be wasted if I went into art; it would be better if I made working drawings of diesel engines. My dear mother knew better, and my father had been dead since I was eleven but I think that he would have sided with mother in this judgment call; he was elected class poet by his eighth grade graduating class and, in my earliest memory, had one of her Chicago pastels framed and hanging in the living room.

So, there was little doubt about my calling. My stint in the Air Force was a matter of special circumstances, and when that was finished, art would take its place.

7

Montbartier

We flew our sixth mission on June 25, and it was sharply memorable for reasons in addition to enemy action. It was deep into southern France to a place called Montbartier, actually little more than a village. The Germans, however, had a massive underground oil-storage facility there, but it was well hidden. We were to bomb by a triangulation of checkpoints using deep-penetrating bombs. This was still a technical matter for the lead teams. I was, as yet, the guy on my crew who kept track of where we were and how we were faring on our schedule.

By this time, we were considered an experienced crew, and Porter was placed as an instructor with a new crew, while their copilot was assigned to ride with us. He was a small, bright-eyed young man who looked little more than seventeen. We later learned that he had come right out of twin-engine school and had had little, if any, B-17 transition training, and we could only wonder why he had been placed on that crew. Anyway, somewhere over the middle of France, while he was taking his turn at the yoke and throttles, the problems of high-altitude formation flying proved too much for him, and he lost control. We had been tucked into the left side and behind the lead plane of our element; and since, as copilot, he was in the right seat where he had the most direct view, he had been allowed to get some experience.

Things happened fast. I was enjoying the view from the nose bowl, and perhaps John was dozing a little in the warming sunshine, when I noticed that we were gaining rapidly on our element lead and drifting over toward him. I was really alarmed to see that the process was going unchecked and that in another moment our engines were going to chew right into his tail. It looked as if the tip of his left stabilizer was within touching distance when I yelled at the top of my voice to Lockhart. He responded with an instantaneous pull-up and sharp bank to the left. The heavily loaded bird almost stalled, and down we went in a steep spiral, very nearly a spin. It must have been an especially wild ride for our crew aft of the bomb bay. I could imagine heavy ammo boxes flying around like loose cannons. We plunged down almost a thousand feet before order was restored and Russell set about catching the formation and gaining the altitude to fit back into our notch. This required a substantially increased power setting with a considerably greater fuel burn, and since this was a long mission, there was concern about our total supply. We did catch up, however, and participated normally on the bomb run.

After some unaccountable changes of course, we left coast-out south of Bordeaux, where we ran into extremely bad weather over the Bay of Biscay and were forced to disengage from the formation. Since visibility dropped to nearly zero, the group leader ordered us to descend carefully to the deck. Down, slowly, down we dropped while my altimeter gradually unwound. There were no other planes in sight, and when we reached 1,000 feet above sea level there was nothing to see but a dark dense fog, up, down, and sideways. Russ had made the descent on autopilot to maintain an accurate heading and to rest his weary arms. Our copilot was simply a humble passenger. We decided to feel our way down a little further in search of at least a bit of visibility, thus reducing the danger of collision. At 200 feet an indistinct darkness below was the first indication of the surface. At 100 feet black waves with muddy-gray white-caps were visible, although barely.

After a while Russ let her settle a little more. The sea looked frightening, although there was not as much air turbulence as I had expected. There were ragged patches of fog that occasionally extended all the way to the surface; but since there were thirty-five other B-17s somewhere near, we had no choice but to continue by visual contact, and Russell couldn't use the autopilot with so little altitude available. My room with a view was at best a mixed blessing since I had always ranked sea tragedies among my favorite horror stories when I was a child. But the reality of those slate-colored waves so close that I could see their small angular surface patterns had me in a sweat.

In my brief intercom conferences with Russell about our position and ETA, he seemed calm and settled for a long haul. Certainly his strength and mettle as a pilot was tested and proven during the rest of our flight; and since he could not trust his copilot for periods of relief, those must have been long hours. But at this point, without the necessity of formation flying and its throttle jockeying, which consumes more fuel, he was able to reduce our power setting to a very economical burn. We at least were in less danger of running out of gas.

From that point I had to earn my keep as a navigator, and without my Gee set, part of which was in the radio shop. It was the first time in my life that my responsibility was total and inescapable. Fortunately I had kept an airplot very carefully on my Mercator, so with the last-known wind vector applied I had a fair idea of our position. The metro wind prediction for our flight south over France had turned out to be quite accurate, so I assumed that at our planned altitude it might also be true. But at sea level the wind would be somewhat slower and shifted a bit counterclockwise. This seemed to be the case when I compared the direction of the white-cap streaks over the waves with our compass heading. Our wind at altitude was expected to be 295 degrees at forty-six knots; and while the waves were impressive to my unpracticed eye, the wind moving them was certainly considerably less, perhaps half of that, and the direction seemed to be more like 240 degrees. I decided to use that observation for my wind vector and altered my airplot accordingly. I gave Russell a heading that would safely clear the Brest peninsula and figured an estimated time for course change that would bring us in near Plymouth. After that, with time to throw away, I pealed down to let the sweat evaporate. My mask hung from its strap, and I held it to my face only when I had to use the mike. Jardine had all but stripped, and was on at least his third cigarette.

"OK, Robert," he might have said, "I hope you paid attention at navigation school. This looks like a good final exam."

I probably replied, "I had to, my instructor was cruel."

I chewed on my pencil for want of a cigarette, and hoped that we wouldn't run into a ship.

The hours dragged by while we seemed to be suspended in a strange dream. Nothing changed except for one course alteration after we had gotten beyond the Brest peninsula. Finally the waves became merely monotonous rather than frightening. John seemed to be off in the land of nod, and I let my mind suspend operations except for an infrequent glance at my watch. In effect, I had set a mental alarm clock for the coast-in ETA. Russell was bearing the load of this 600-mile stress test fifty feet above the billows, and I was thankful for his unwavering toughness.

Finally, as we neared my guess for coast-in, the fog mercifully began to thin a little, allowing us to see the cliffs in time to climb without having to make a panic pull-up. We had some distance yet to go in murky weather, but as we angled up the side of a green hill, I felt like we were home again, with such mundane things to notice as a stomach growling with hunger pangs, and when Russell asked me for a heading and ETA to Deenethorpe, he was slightly irritated by my failure to answer in thirty seconds. I guess he was tired and in no mood for my laziness, and then too, he probably had an apprehensive eye on the fuel gauges. This flight was going to come to nearly ten hours.

At the hardstand we were met by the group photographer who wanted to take our crew picture for a news release. It was the usual,

Our crew after Montbartier and Bay Biscay, June 25, 1944. *Back row, from left:* novice copilot, Russell Lockhart, John Jardine, Jay Karper, and Elno Pyles. *Front row:* Ray Miller, Larry Million, Otto Schlaegel, Lloyd Null, and Robert Grilley.

with the back row standing and front row sitting or kneeling, but this time we were each asked to hold up the palms of our hands with all fingers showing. With ten of us it made an even hundred, and it, we were told, signified that this had been the hundredth mission of the group. For us it had been nearly ten hours in the air, and a difficult ten, but in the photo we all look like it had been a day in the country. We smile out of that picture from nearly sixty years ago as if we were having the time of our lives. I have an 8 x 10 of it in my studio and look at it occasionally, marveling at the resilience of youth. There is a sad epilogue to this little narrative, though. Our bright-eyed young guest copilot was killed with his crew a few weeks later when his plane was hit and blown up in a ball of flame. There were no survivors.

8

Leipzig I

July 7, 1944, 0100 hours by my watch, the earliest yet, number eight; twenty-seven more after this one. I probably did the arithmetic while counting sheep. Jardine was really mad. "Gedowdahere," he roared at the flashlight, loud enough to finish the wake-up call, and Russell set him off again with the same old stuff. "Hey John, didn't they ever tell you not to volunteer?"

It was a set piece for John. "Aw, Lockhart, fer Christsake, knock it off," he groaned after blowing his nose. "Just one more time, and that's it."

"That's what?" asked Russell.

Considering the ridiculous hour, speculation suggested Munich, but it turned out to be Leipzig, way the hell and gone over there, almost as far as Munich and twice as bad. Munich was a sentimental place for the Nazis' founding fathers, like Philadelphia is for us Americans, and worthy of sharp-tracking flak. But Leipzig was big business; aircraft and oil, and part of the Merseburg ring, a whole different ballgame. Somebody wouldn't come back. The flak would be a thousand-gun box barrage with lots of 105s that made explosions the size of two-car garages.

Bombing strike, aircraft assembly plant, Leipzig.

At the crew chief's tent I tuned out the grousing and fondled the thought of Leipzig as art; a late-medieval town with tall Gothic churches, one where Johann Sebastian Bach played out his final years and where Mendelssohn dug him out of his musical grave and presented him to the world; better a concert maybe than a bomb run.

But our target was not actually Leipzig. We were going to knock down an aircraft assembly plant outside of town where they made parts underground and put them together in cheaply made sheds. The P-38 recon photos showed a nearby runway they used to fly them away; altogether a rather attractive job from our employer's point of view.

It was a midsummer's clear day, and according to metro it would be all the way across Germany. Forming-up would be painless, even pretty. Coast-out would be Lowestoft, with coast-in at Dokkum in the north of Holland, where the Dutch would certainly be cheering for us, but quietly, very quietly.

Leipzig is eighty-five miles southwest of Berlin, overland almost all the way, where they could spring all kinds of surprises on you, like a new jet fighter, the Me 262, first I'd ever heard of. It could fly circles around a Mustang, but didn't have much range. Even so, if your group was the one they were practicing on, look out!

Our IP was at Stassfurt, thirty-five miles north of the target, and our formation was already good and tight both for fighter defense and a concentrated bomb strike. If our lead bombardier was hot, we'd really wipe the place out; if he wasn't, all our bombs would be in a cornfield a mile away. A loose formation would put some on and some off, but Bowman wouldn't settle for that. We were one of the top teams in the majors, and our leads had the best circular error rate in the Eighth.

As promised, the flak was violent. The 105s could really scare you, but even the 88s, of which there were more, could kill you with one potshot. Our formation was a group commander's dream, but risky in a way. If your neighbor took a direct hit and blew up, he could bring you down with him. But since our whole purpose for being there was to take out the factory sheds and runway, with nothing but our solipsisms making any personal promises, there was nowhere to go but forward. It was great-grandpa Henry Cruger's frontal assault at Vicksburg all over again.

Jardine, since we were following the leader, kept his eye on their open bomb bay and his finger on the salvo switch and, after what seemed like a whole combat tour, bellowed "Bombs away!"

We lost three plane; nothing horrendous, well within the normal range, which had a biological equivalent. The loss of particular individuals was an inconsequential consideration unless they exceeded a percentage that would threaten the survival of the species.

And I should also tell you that we did get a "shack" which bombardier cadets called the little wooden structure at the center of their training targets out in the sands of New Mexico. That is to say, our strike photos were right on, better than 90 percent, virtually perfect. Regrettably, we may have killed some slave laborers. I hope not. I truly hope not.

9

Munich I and II

After the aircraft factory raid at Leipzig on July 7, we, the 613th, had four days free. The rest of the group went somewhere on one of those days, but this was our day of stand-down by rotation among the four squadrons. The weather was clear to partly cloudy, and there was a warm wind from the south. Each day in the late afternoon, tall picture-making cumulus clouds built to enormous heights where, taking the full intensity of the sun on their western sides, they certainly were the whitest things in the world. By contrast, the sky was a deeper blue and the Landscape a darker green. It all had the look of painter's drawings, so I used warm gray paper from Winsor & Newton and worked with black and iron-oxide red pencils, using fine-grained white chalk to heighten the brightest parts of the clouds and long patches of light that flowed in the fields beyond pools of shadows from hills and trees. So well were they developing that had they been expertly matted and framed in antiqued gold leaf; they could almost have been taken for seventeenth-century, that is, with some imitation fox markings.

But while I had been drawing from nature by concentrated observation, I'd really been drawing from nature through the eyes of Baroque artists. I excused my eclecticism by reminding myself that learning by imitation was how it had always been done, until modernism

took the bit in its teeth, and that if you had a seed of originality waiting inside to germinate, it would when it was good and ready.

Elizabeth came to visit after an interval of several days. I'd gotten
used to her, like something in nature that is remarkable only by its
absence, and realized that, indulgent as it might seem, I had come to
see her as a pleasant contrast to mission madness. I was glad to see
her and even presumed to wonder where she'd been—on her knees
digging in the garden or flying on her long-roped swing or sitting at
the kitchen table cutting things out of prewar catalogs; though she
might simply have gone somewhere with her mom, maybe to visit
friends in Kettering.

I'd not drawn her in a while, as she effortlessly reminded me. It
seemed, although she didn't say so, that I could draw trees and clouds
any day when it was not raining, but she was there and available for
picture making at that time and place, a serious drawing on the best
handmade paper that money could buy—not as an idealized peasant
girl, à la Bouguereau; instead as realism, Bastien-Lepage on-the-spot
realism, and yet maybe not; there was a curiously old-fashioned look
about her. Except that she was always barefoot and so lightly dressed,
she reminded me of the best children's book illustrations done in the
1920s by draftsmen with clear eyes and good hands. As a student the
figure and portrait had been my choice, and here was a fine subject. I
could look to the youthful Degas for a suggestion. Elizabeth had the
well-molded child's face that he would have liked, a light-colored
Hortense Valpençon. A serious drawing then, not a freehand sketch.
I would use warm-gray toned paper and heighten it with white, altogether suitable for matting and framing; it would be head, neck, and
shoulders, allowing her a perfectly unposed rotation and tilt, a semi-
profile of fine proportion; and of course there it was, she always surprised me, so unselfconsciously did she make the picture for me.

On the evening of July 11, after my several days in the Landscape, we
were posted again, and *der Totentanz* would begin again—how
early? After part of a fitful night, we would see.

July 12. Mission ten. The wake-up caller was a different guy this time. Someone strangled the other one? No, we were disappointed with the news that our regular would be back in a day or so—just a bout with stomach flu, or maybe a bottle too many.

We had a fine breakfast, Canadian bacon and fresh eggs. Sometimes it seemed that they couldn't do enough for us—plenty for seconds or thirds or all you could eat. There was even a lot of loud, lighthearted talk and yelling. Maybe we were a bunch of manic-depressives in our manic stage for no reason—up at 0100 hours surely meant that we'd not be daisy-cutting in France. They even hung a different-shaped map to tell us where we were going.

It was Munich, the old beer hall putsch place, Hitler's own fabled home town. Maybe we'd bomb a brewery, and beer would be running in the streets. Not really, it was some kind of an ordinance plant—where we would blow up a bunch of 105s, or even 88s, or for that matter, anything they could use against us.

"Do it men, and it will seriously hurt the enemy," Bowman intoned. Well, that's what we always did, hit them right where it hurt the most. As a matter of fact, the 401st had an exceptionally good CE record, printed clearly in *Impact* magazine. Who should doubt?

Munich was a long ride, way down into southeastern Germany, further from home than I'd ever been before. The good news, if there was any, was that the flak was supposed to be a little lighter there than at our previous big jobs. But what about fighters? Would they have a free run? No one said that the Mustangs could get all the way down there.

We took off at 0421 hours, up through light morning clouds, up and out of them quickly. Coast-out was Beachy Head, and coast in was again St. Valéry-en-Caux, the old familiar road to Paris. In fact, we stayed in France all the way to Strasbourg before crossing the border into Germany. The next check points were Ulm and Neu Ulm, and still no fighters. Then we made a slight, slow turn to the initial point at Landsburg on the Lech river. The bomb run was only thirty-six miles long, and with a strong tail wind that wouldn't take more than seven minutes.

Already it was obvious that the Germans were using tracking flak rather than a barrage, but as we got in closer, near the north end of a long scenic lake, I could tell that these gunners had been to school somewhere, and knew what they were doing. One of the B-17s in the 615th had been hit and was smoking conspicuously.

But God almighty, something crazy was happening. The whole group was turning without dropping—and there was the reason, one of the other groups from the 94th Wing was crossing over in front of us. It was like two galaxies on a collision course. Russell came on, paused a moment, and said that we were going home and that we should drop anywhere along our course while we were still in Germany.

As soon, then, as we were completely out of our turn, and on a 290-degree heading, John checked to see that the low squadron was not under us and hit the salvo switch, mumbling, "Bombs dropped."

After a minute or less, Null came on and said that somebody's bombs had hit a small town and that other bomb ripples were going off all over the place—everybody was getting rid of them as soon as possible. What a bloody screw-up. Somebody would be shot for this, if they still did that sort of thing.

It took nearly five painful hours to get back to Deenethorp. We were not hit by fighters, but I saw no Mustangs around and expected an attack at any time—I felt tired and on edge. The engines seemed to vibrate louder. The head wind cut our ground speed by quite a bit, and even the sun, which was right overhead, seemed to glare more that usual. The minute hand on my watch hardly moved, and the hour hand was stuck dead. It was like waiting for spring on the coldest day in January.

We went back through France by nearly the same route and coasted in at Beachy Head. The thin broken clouds were closing for the most part to solid. My Gee box was useful, and we were right on line for runway two-three.

Of course, interrogation was bedlam, and I was glad to have my two shots of Irish and head for the chow hall. I wondered if we would get credit for the mission, but Russell said he was assured that we would, though he agreed that we'd probably have a return engagement.

While we were walking back it started to sprinkle, not really rain, just a drop on the nose or the hand every now and then. Porter said he was going to write this thing up in his little notebook right away, and he wanted to use my map of Europe, the one pinned over my bed. I said I'd do the same thing this evening since we were not posted.

I felt trashed. We'd been in the air for more than nine hours, alien air bristling with hate, with nothing to show for it except, as I pointed out to myself, one mission closer to a long happy life. I took my big black English umbrella, although it was not at the moment raining, and headed for the Landscape. There was a little grassy rise on the hillside under the largest oak where I'd found the right view, sun or rain, and it was there that I dropped down to wait—for what, I wasn't sure. Possibly for some kind of peace to descend on me.

The breeze had freshened a bit, and little flecks of rain were slanting in under the leaves, but there was no need yet for the umbrella. The barley, beginning to turn yellow, was visible beyond the hedge, and it waved rhythmically in the wind with a never-repeating pattern. It had become a kind of visual music for me, complex yet subtle, and, in a sense, my mind could listen to it.

Four days later, on a bright, sunny day, we went back to Munich, as I supposed we would. We used the same route again. You couldn't fool the Germans, so why try? They'd do whatever they could about it, and they did up the price with increasingly intense flak. Their fighters had less fuel, so it became for them, a gradually more difficult vectoring problem.

This time we seemed to have hit the target, at least what was supposed to be the target, and nobody was shot down, although the tracking flak chewed us up more, it seemed, than it did last time. It still took over nine hours—probably four or five of those spent in a thirty-two-pound flak suit, depending on how brave you were. Of course, after Hamburg I was quite a dedicated user, even though two or three hours in one was a backbreaker. I suppose it squashed my disks a little.

It was still a nice day when we got back, and interrogation was less hectic. The beautiful Red Cross girl gave us frosted doughnuts and coffee with canned milk. Was she there last time? I couldn't even remember. I only took one shot of Irish because I was tired—fatigued, not a nervous wreck.

Most of the guys went to the club, as they often did after a long one, and finished off with Scotch. There was no mission posted, so the green light over the bar would stay on until 0200 hours, although anyone gotten up at one o'clock would never have made it past ten.

I went to the Landscape.

10

Leipzig II

July 20, 0100 hours. It would be Germany again. After the flashlight Jardine wasn't as noisy as usual. He sat on his bed dragging on a Camel and hawking up phlegm.

"Hey John, you sick?" asked Murgatroyd. "Say something."

Jardine raised his right arm in a fascist salute, cigarette between his thumb and index finger, and droned, "Dolce et decorum est pro patria mori."

"Christsake, what's that?" Ken asked.

"It's sweet and beautiful to die for one's country."

"The hell you say," responded Russell. "What kinda mumbo's that?"

John was in his drawling intellectual mode. "If you guys had even a modicum of education you'd know it's Latin. Any English public school boy could tell you that, and also that Latin builds moral fiber. The RAF relies on it."

"Relies on what?"

"Moral fiber. It gives their Lancs longer range."

"So, whadda they need us for? I get my fiber from bran flakes," said somebody.

At briefing there was a lot of snuffling and coughing. Everybody got up too early; not a healthy thing, all that chilly English mist.

It was Leipzig, another one of those death-defying stunts our country kept asking us to do. I really liked Bowman, but I wasn't always happy with what he had to say, although sometimes his euphemisms could be delightful. "Our efforts today will help wean the enemy from his insatiable oil habit."

After that, it was a matter of specific details left to the briefing people; target photos, flak maps, weather, escape advice, etc. And finally some last paternal words from Bowman. Everybody liked him. We could piss and moan all we wanted. He'd even banter with us to help lighten up. We'd go to the ends of the earth and back for him, and often we did.

As I've complained before, Leipzig was all the way across the endless middle of Germany. You couldn't just dash in for a quick hit and run. It was a marathon. Metro said we'd have a strong wind from the northwest, and my airplot showed it to be true. We were doing better than 280, but coming back against it would be a real athletic event.

Our IP was a little lake at Waldheim twenty five miles to the southeast for a bomb run straight back into a head wind, slow, with no drift, good for bomb aiming but bad for the health.

We lost three planes in short order, one from each box. Murgatroyd's was the one from ours. It took what appeared to be a direct hit and came apart in large sections with a lot of smoke and flame and passed back out of my sight. Null in the ball and Million in the tail got the final view and reported nobody out, but they qualified that by saying there was so much debris it was hard to tell.

I was stunned. I'd already seen a variety of shoot-downs, but this was something else. These were guys we lived with, ate and drank with, shot the bull with. They showed us their dirty French postcards from London and shared their cookies from home and snored in our ears before the flashlight and groused when they woke up; pretty sentimental stuff.

Jardine howled bombs-away, so I had to pay attention and get back to my airplot readings and log entries.

The empty places in the echelons closed up quickly, and we turned straight north to get out of the Merseburg-Leipzig flak ring as soon as possible, then to a heading of 290 degree average for the long haul, having to zigzag around the known flak zones and blundering into the unknown ones.

After all the babble at interrogation, none of it making Ken's shootdown any clearer, I was ready for my two Irish doubles and whatever there was for chow.

At the table with Porter there wasn't much to say. I kept seeing grainy newsreels in my head, rerun after rerun until all of them I'd ever seen came together in one big soundless bright spot with debris expanding away from it like some cosmic event.

At the exit of the chow hall a large notice was posted telling us that Marlene Dietrich would put on a USO show on the afternoon of July 22 at 1700 hours. I guess we needed that. I thought of *The Blue Angel* in detail, and some of her other masterpieces. Her marvelous German accent would be the perfect irony, something to savor.

When I was passing the farmyard, Lispeth came walking a line of interception to meet me.

"My mum likes the new draw'n of me even better than the first one," she said with what almost amounted to a smile. "I furgot to tell you last time. She thinks if sometime you would, would you drawr me with shoes on?"

"Never saw you with shoes on—do you have some?" I asked as we walked.

"Oh, you," she hissed, scowling up at me.

"It's not going to rain, tomorrow—how about then?"

"Well, okay, I'll tell her," she said, dropping down on the grass and rolling down the slope.

It was beginning to look like Lispeth's mysterious mother was a drawing collector.

She was waiting in the yard when I arrived for our "sitting," or "standing," or whatever it turned out to be. I could see that her mother had made an effort. Clearly Lispeth had been scrubbed, and there had been an attempt to make some order in the erstwhile tangle of her tow-colored hair. She was wearing a starchy-clean, somewhat outgrown gray-blue dress with short gathered shoulder sleeves. She had on remarkably white anklets and black patent-leather slippers that were unscuffed. They must have pinched, though, because somehow they didn't seem to be as large as her bare feet; but when she walked there was no sign that they gave her discomfort. She was holding a lightweight hemispherical hat with a narrow brim, which she gingerly placed on her head, pushing it around to find a fit.

"My mum says that you might want to use this," she offered without enthusiasm.

"What do you think?" I asked.

"Naw, less you want to."

"It might help to keep you from squinting," I suggested.

"Naw, if we go in the shade," was her firmed-up opinion.

"Let's try you sitting and then standing to see what'll work," I said, dragging one of the weathered wooden boxes into the shade of the stone wall. "Sit with your hands in your lap," I commanded. She did it right the first time, as I expected, so I brought over another box for myself and began.

"Where's your mom?" I asked.

"Oh, she's out in the back garden. Gram is canning a lot, and she's getting it all in."

The drawing turned out quite well; actually I'd like to have kept it, but I thought of it as a model fee, and I had several other very good ones of her barefoot.

11

Marlene Dietrich

It didn't do much good to get to the Marlene Dietrich show early. There were no seats, and the crowd was quite fluid. You naturally expected to stand and to move about as the current flowed. She was going to arrive in Colonel Bowman's well-polished B-17 and climb down a little aluminum ladder from the front hatch, and we were all hoping that she would be wearing a short silk skirt like she did in *The Blue Angel.*

At about ten minutes to five, the plane taxied up close, and engines one and four were cut. As soon as the props stopped, the hatch dropped open, and the earsplitting roar of the lusty crowd could be heard, I'd guess, quite distinctly in the village. But there was disappointment, deep disappointment. The most beautiful legs in the whole world were sedately covered by tan gabardine slacks, and even the little breeze that everyone was counting on was wasted.

She was wearing a chamois helmet and aviation goggles pushed up on her forehead—for show, of course—and when she reached the ground she pulled them off and shook her curly locks with a graceful tilt of that most lovely head.

Colonel Bowman went through an unnecessary introduction, but even the PA system was overwhelmed. Then, in spite of the total disorder, Dietrich stepped to the microphone and the colonel yelled for everybody to shut up. At first she spoke to us in her deep, husky version of English, and then she switched to German. God, what a beautiful language. How could our cruel enemies have such a native tongue? But the answer was, of course, that they couldn't make it sound like that.

Then she sang, and even with a tinny piano behind her, the air changed to antique gold dust.

"Just see what the boys in the back room will have, and tell them I died of the same," she crooned, with a gesture and wink worth a million bucks.

Everybody screamed their throats raw, and after an hour the likes of which none of us would ever hear again, she finished in splendor with the saddest, most beautiful song to be heard anywhere in that year of 1944—"Lili Marlene," the favorite of the Luftwaffe and probably all German males past puberty, including flak gunners. I had to admit that when it came to such things, they may have had superior taste.

12

Saint-Lô

The Eighth Air Force high command and its chain of subordinate unit commanders made no special effort to keep us informed about the progress of the war. Except for Bowman's exhortations at briefing about destroying the enemy's sources and supplies of war matériel, little was said about how our actions fit into the big picture. In general, I could keep abreast through reports in the London papers, although I had more than a strong suspicion that there was a biased spin given to some of them in favor of Montgomery—but at least we were on the same side. The *Stars and Stripes* was also of some value, but in a different way, sometimes even a humorous one.

Usually we welcomed an occasional tactical mission to attack German ground forces, which, compared with the hardship and danger of our long strategic flights, could be done with dispatch and relative impunity. Sometimes, though, we even found that our intervention had made a major contribution, and while the mass killing of German soldiers seemed somehow more conspicuously brutal than the destruction of factories, where I liked to delude myself that the workers were safe in bomb shelters, it was certain that we saved a great number of our own and helped to hasten the final collapse of the Wehrmacht in Normandy.

Our thirteenth and fourteenth missions, flown on July 24 and 25, were to Saint-Lô, where heavy German armored units were still strong and stubborn and capable of inflicting lethal damage on a broad front. We, of the Eighth, were called on to lay down the equivalent of the most massive artillery barrage ever conceived; and as it transpired it became a rain of fire and steel without precedent in the annals of human conflict, so huge in fact, that part of its fury overlapped our own forces.

As a participant, I'm drawn to a look back through the long tunnel of time to see the totality of what happened.

Earthbound witnesses viewed it as virtually a supernatural event. Ernie Pyle reported to his rapt American readers that the "march across the sky was slow and studied. I've never known a storm, or machine, or any resolve of man that had about it the aura of such ghastly relentlessness. You had the feeling that even had God appeared beseechingly before them in the sky with palms outward to persuade them back, they would not have had within them the power to turn from their irresistible course."

The lines beyond which we were to deliver our massive strike were to be designated by yellow smoke markers. However, a temporary wind shift falsified some of them, and a group dropped short, killing 111 of our men, including Lieutenant General Lesley McNair, and wounding several hundred more.

There was much bitterness among those who suffered this catastrophe. I learned about it only after the whole event could be told and put in perspective.

Our sector had no such problem, and we received an official commendation for our strike on the 25th. In fact, our total effort was, on balance, a tremendous success, and entire German divisions were devastated, so the offensive was carried out as planned with far fewer casualties than would have been possible without our strike. It was Patton's famous breakthrough and blitz.

The crack German Panzer Lehr Division, formerly considered invincible, received its coup de grâce, and its commander, General Fritz Bayerlein, reported, "By noon nothing was visible but dust and smoke. My front lines looked like the face of the moon and at least 70 percent of my troops were knocked out—dead, wounded, crazed or numbed" (John Keegan, *The Times Atlas of the Second World War* [London: *Times* Books, 1989], 393).

We got back from the killing fields early in the day, and, of all people, Jardine hailed me as we were coming out of the chow hall and invited me to the club for a drink or two. Well, what was this? In a sense I was flattered. He usually spent his long afternoons, evenings, and nights when we were not posted with the most celebrated drunks at Deenethorpe, so I was just a little curious about the occasion or purpose of this honor. He had had three long shots of Irish at interrogation, while I had learned to be satisfied with one, but I could nurse a Scotch or two for social purposes, and soon we each had a cold wet one in hand.

"Well, Robert, what didja think of that?"

It seemed he'd asked the same question once before on our way back from Paris, but with a smile that time.

"I wouldn't want to make it my life's work," said I.

"Naw, I mean really, what didja think of that?"

"What do you mean, what did I think of it?"

"Aw for Christsake, you know what I mean. That was a friggin' slaughter pen."

"Jesus, John, did you drag me in here just to discuss the immorality of war? I'm not a born killer, but I can't think of any way to stop this thing with diplomacy. It's gotten down to the point where may the best man win, and I hope it's me."

"It was a friggin' slaughter," he moaned.

"Well, I'm not an eye-for-an-eye disciple, but if we have to kill German soldiers to get this Goddamned thing over, so be it. You think our mud-faced GIs have to do it all? D'ya think that Hitler is responsible for it; I mean, that he just tells them what to do, and they just go out and do it? There's more to it than that. The German people were all for it when they were winning big."

"You're talking so much, you haven't touched your drink," John observed. "Listen, Robert, you don't have to get so worked up. I simply said it was a hell of a slaughter."

"OK, I agree, and I get pretty sad about the whole thing sometimes. What more can I say?"

"Hey, Robert, to change the subject: What the hell do you do with yourself all the time? I never see you around."

"Well, funny thing, John, I was going to ask you the same thing, but since you asked first, I'll tell you. I'm doing a lot of drawing."

"Drawing. Drawing of what?"

"The landscapes out behind our hut. I even call the place 'the Landscape,' with a capital L. And also an eight-year-old girl who lives at the farm a hundred yards from our door. I got some of the best handmade paper and drawing materials in the world from Winsor & Newton in London."

"Well I knew you were a university grad and an art afficionado, but what the hell, why not? Drink up and have another. But how'd you find this young model?"

"I didn't. She actually found me drawing on their place. You know, John, we've been in a B-17 a lot of hours together, and you act like we've just been introduced."

"Well, I guess we just have," he mumbled.

13

Merseburg

July 28, mission fifteen. We got the flashlight in the face very early again. It would be somewhere way over there. There wasn't a whole lot of table talk at breakfast, but the sunny-side eggs were temporary bright spots in the gloom. We'd had a run on the green powder scrambled stuff and were in need of a little diversion. I managed to get three and some not-too-greasy hash browns, powdered milk with just a touch of coffee in it—at a little under room temperature—and a lot of syrupy canned peaches.

At briefing the air was heavy, and there was a dense low overcast of cigarette smoke. Background grumbling blended with the scraping of chairs on the concrete floor. Someone released the tension a bit with a loud and remarkably protracted belch, which brought on a similar one in answer. There was a lot of stretching and yawning and scratching, which reminded me of apprehensive dogs; and the breaking of wind here and there came with defiant smiles that seemed to say, "Better here than up there in somebody's ox regulator."

"Tenn-hut," and in strode Colonel Bowman.

"At ease, gentlemen. Today you will strike a major blow (sounds ominous) against the enemy's ability to fuel his machines of war. The Leüna oil-from-coal plant at Merseburg is their largest and most productive. It's been hit and damaged before, but they've got it back in full working order again, all ready for your serious attention. The whole world, as we want it to be, is depending on you. Remember, oil is as important as gunpowder in this war."

The curtain had been drawn just as the colonel put us at ease, and I'm sure that no one in the room was able to attain that blessed state. It was a long way across Germany, and the Leipzig-Merseburg area had the reputation of being a snake pit.

Dümmer Lake was a checkpoint of turn some seventy miles beyond the Netherlands border. We were there right on the minute and began a slow course change to 160 degrees mag heading to avoid the Hanover flak zone. Lakes were good checkpoints, if there happened to be any along the way, for the simple reason that there were so few. This particular lake was egg shaped with a north-south axis, and it appeared to have smooth beaches on the eastern edge. To the west it seemed marshy with low scrubby woods, and was not at all unlike a large pond in central Wisconsin. A small river called the Hunte ran through a very inconspicuous town with the perfect German name Diepholz and then into Dümmer Lake—all of it way out in the sticks—no one would expect to be bombed there. Maybe kids, refugee kids from the war cities might be there swimming or fishing from the shore. Except for the Nazis, Germany would be an interesting place to go hiking or biking, and my guess was that they made much better beer than they did in Milwaukee. Also, I would have bet that most of the people could have looked you right in the eye and told you that they were against the war and if the Nazis had not been able to blame the Versailles treaty, there never would have been this terrible misunderstanding.

Our IP at the small city of Muhlhausen lay along that heading. We covered the distance in thirty-eight minutes and turned slightly short for a tighter formation. The bomb run of sixty-eight miles on a course of about 80 degrees gave us an almost direct tailwind, so we were really flying—literally and figuratively. It was quite obvious that the faster you flew through a box barrage, the better your chances were for survival because they could only fire a set number of shells per minute; and since Merseburg could bring more than a thousand heavy guns to bear, many of them 105 mms, it was wise to plan for a tailwind. The other side of this coin was that bombing accuracy might be somewhat compromised by excessive speed.

About forty miles out we could see a sizable smudge of dark smoke at the target area, so it was clear that the group ahead of us had hit something. But God, there they were, the fields of black shell bursts right at our altitude. At twenty miles out we were entering the valley. It was going to be "The Charge of the Light Brigade" all over again. Alfred Lord Tennyson; I wondered if he'd ever heard a shot fired in anger, and what was so gallant about 600 guys in red coats waving sabers riding horseback into a valley full of live cannons? The Victorians had a thing about it—getting their heads blown off vicariously in poetry. "Just Before the Battle, Mother" fit my mood better.

Flak. It'd be a solar eclipse—a thunder and lightning storm—iron hail. My thirty-two-pound flak suit was tissue paper, and my big steel helmet was like a woman's bathing cap. Christ, this would be worse than Hamburg.

At four and a half miles a minute or more, we'd be in it for almost five minutes until bomb release, and after that they'd keep chasing us for maybe three or four minutes.

The dark things got bigger and bigger and blacker and blacker, some with orange centers, and they were sliding past faster and faster, which meant closer and closer. I could hear the high-pitched crack of the explosions and feel the concussions rattling the whole ship. Jardine was hunched forward, either trying to bring his helmet as close to the shoulders of his flak suit as possible or studying the smoking target that was becoming more clearly visible. I dropped to my knees beside him to see this thing, but what remains in my mind's eye flickers like an old newsreel. It seems to be a dark patch of long interconnected structures—maybe images from the bombing scene in *Hell's Angels*.

"Three minutes to release," I called over the intercom, and "Yes, the bomb bay doors were open." Then lightning struck with an intense simultaneous *crack!* Old Bird seemed to bounce up from a gigantic pothole in the road, and the ventilation suddenly increased by triple. Shards of Plexiglas clattered back against the bulkhead, driven by spears of 150 mile an hour indicated air speed. The nose bowl had several holes up to two inches, a massive split—Jardine, you okay? Yes, okay. Jesusss, we were full of holes, and in some places the metal skin was peeled back. My Mercator was flapping around in the subzero breeze, and my log was over in the corner. I pulled my goggles down where they should have been and grabbed two or three times for my log. More sharp cracks, and I contracted like a turtle. We were going to get it; we were going to; then I could see that somebody really had gotten it. They were burning from the whole right side and banking into a climbing half-roll right up over us. The astrodome was full of bright-orange light.

"Bombs away!" howled Jardine, and the ship floated up for a moment until Lockhart wound in some nose down trim.

We turned left pretty fast, fast enough to loosen up the formation. The flak had almost stopped at the release point. It was the eye of the hurricane, but in a minute or so it was banging away again, and there was another plane blazing bright over in the 615th. There were two or three bail-outs, little specks drifting down and away, and then it flopped over and nosed down, down, in a slow-motion spin.

I got back to business again and entered most of these things in my log with rather shaky printing, holding it down in the wind as best I could. The flak gradually died away, and the sun came out again. Now what? Fighters? This was going to be long, and we weren't even halfway through. Old Ulio'd be sending out a yellow snowstorm of telegrams.

We got back to Deenethorpe frazzled and frozen after eight hours and thirty-two minutes air time. Interrogation dragged out as usual with a lot of very subjective narratives. I accepted a second long shot of Irish whiskey from the flight surgeon's man and ate chow without a lot of enthusiasm.

July 29, mission sixteen—why didn't the Germans just give up? They were going to lose anyway, and it could have saved us a whole hell of a lot of trouble.

That was the second day in a row, like Hamburg and Berlin, and another one o'clock reveille. The generals who planned these things were putting us on notice that business was business. Even Jardine was quiet while we were pulling on our socks. Breakfast was a rather sullen affair. A lot of guys smoked between bites, and there weren't many graveyard jokes.

Waiting for the colonel at briefing was hard on my nerves. I was beginning to think that those ARMA psychologists had overestimated me and was relieved when "Tenn-hut" was yelled.

"At ease," said Colonel Bowman as the curtain was swept aside, and Goddamn, there it was again. Merseburg! The one place in the whole world that I never ever wanted to see again.

"Gentlemen," he raised his hand to shush us, "you did a great job yesterday, and I congratulate you. Unfortunately, it's the enemy's largest and most extensive facility of its kind, and some work yet remains to be done. There are many underground tanks that will require deeper penetration. You will each deliver four 1,000-pound deep-diving specials. Burn them out, and the Luftwaffe will be on very short rations. So, guys, go in there and raise hell with 'em!"

The weatherman told us that we'd have another clear summer day with strong southwesterly winds at altitude over eastern Germany. The chaplain prayed for our souls and seemed to ask forgiveness for our transgressions of yesterday; after all, God well knew which side wore the mantle of righteousness. I was thinking more graphically of Dante's Inferno and whether Dante would have liked to make a second trip.

We turned again at Dümmer Lake, with a little more southerly heading this time. Maybe the kids swimming or fishing there looked up, hearing the deep blurred rumble of our engines, but at 27,000 feet we would have been too high to see, and there were no contrails.

Possibly a sharp eye might have picked out some dark specks among the dancing white dots in the cloudless blue.

As we were rolling out of the turn, a flock of FW-190s appeared high at about ten o'clock, and then at about one o'clock another flock of higher-flying fighters showed up. It was hard to tell, but at that distance, they looked like Me-109s. This was going to be another one of those hard days.

But a miracle, Jesus, a true miracle, was starting to happen. The Me-109s were diving at the 190s, and they were turning into Mustangs. Bless your hearts, little friends, bless your hearts.

Our IP was further to the southwest this time, giving us an almost perfect tailwind, but no matter where our bomb run started, they were all set to let us have a full dose. Again, at about twenty miles out, the flak, like a whole army of black headless dwarfs, began to materialize at our altitude, each, by ugly magic, for his killing instant and then hanging there as a gray ghost.

The crew chief and his boys had worked all night to put in a new nose bowl, and I profoundly hoped that they wouldn't have to do it again. The blasts were big and coming by very fast. I could feel the concussions in my chest, and we were rocking from the turbulence. Then, again, right after bomb release, we had that peculiar quiet moment just as we were turning left. But the 105 mms started cracking open again in big clumps in front of us—not hard for them to figure which way we would turn.

After a few minutes the flak began to thin out a little. Maybe we'd have GI drinks and supper at Deenethorpe that evening. But lightning struck again. An ear-splitting *crack* at the Bird's belly, and she lurched upward a moment before settling back level. The wings were still in place, and we still had a tail.

Lockhart called for an all-stations report, and at that instant Karper yelled that the ball had been hit bad and that the whole waist area was full of holes but that he was able to crank the ball into opening position. I could hear fragmentary reports over the intercom that Null was crawling out semi-conscious with blood on his face.

By that time Jardine had managed to work his way back through the bomb bay and radio room with first-aid equipment, and in all haste he administered a shot of morphine. The inch-thick window of the turret had been blown in, and Null's face and eyelids were cut by shards of glass. John was able to delicately tweeze out some of the most painful pieces and apply a special eye ointment. He then remained with his patient by plugging both of their oxygen supply tubes into spare regulators.

The action of the day was not over yet. There was a badly smoking ship on the far side of our squadron, and it was falling back out of sight. Million reported five bail-outs before it twisted over on its back and started its death plunge. The lead box also had a burner that began to drift off in a falling leaflike motion that continued to accelerate. I counted nine out of it, but maybe there was a tenth who couldn't be seen. The G-forces in such a floundering machine must have been violent and irregular, and escape would surely have been a frantic affair.

Our return took us on a more direct westerly route, passing just north of the famous old university city of Göttingen, ancient, but with strong recent research work in the mathematics of airfoil sections. Then, after Münster, that is north of Münster, we passed over into the Netherlands, but we kept most of our altitude because we were still occasionally running into sharp well-aimed tracking flak. After we'd finally passed the Ijesselmeer, our long-awaited letdown began. There was always the quietly joyful feeling when that moment came that life would continue on for a while longer. The engine noise and vibration softened. We were aware of our fatigue, but there was the promise of rest at Deenethorpe, still far over the horizon.

That afternoon after formalities, but before chow, we were happy to find that Lloyd's wounds were not severe and there was no permanent eye damage. Some sutures and patching tape fixed him up fine. He stayed in the hospital a week and was then pronounced fit for duty. Jardine was praised by the doctor for his first-aid care, and we all felt glad.

After eight hours and twenty minutes of air time and a lengthy interrogation, some Irish and chow, it was still only 1700 hours—3:00 o'clock real time—on a remarkably warm day, that is, as English summer days are judged. I was sitting under the oak looking at a small rather frayed book of reproductions of English watercolors. Lispeth found me in less than her usual five minutes and flopped down, cross-legged, hands on her knees. She must have been helping or playing in the garden, because she still had a few chunks of moist mud between the toes of her uncovered foot, and the nails of her evenly spread fingers had thin black crescents under them, perfectly formed as though they'd been painted.

She had been running fast, and her chest heaved for a few moments. There were beads of sweat on her cheek and out-curled upper lip and on the tiny whitish hairs of her forearms. It was late July, and she had become quite tan for a towhead, with eyebrows and eyelashes a pale ochre in contrast, and the light-blueness of her irises even lighter with the blackness of her pupils absolute. She could well have been a Pre-Raphaelite painting, not just a drawing.

"Why do you run that fast on a hot day?"

"Because I like to. It makes it feel cool. Where'd you fly today?"

"Oh, just very high, very, very high."

"But you musta gone somewheres."

"Over the North Sea—you could see Holland."

"But why do you do that?"

"Oh, we're just seeing to it that nothing bad happens."

"Is it part a the war?"

"Yes."

She changed her sitting position from cross-legged to a raised knee with hands back in the grass to natural points of balance, and she looked away at the barley and was quiet for a few moments. Then she asked, "Where'd ya go flying yesterday?"

"Over the North Sea, very high. Out over Lowestoft. There were some small white clouds close together, but you could see the water when you looked down between them."

"Same as today?"

"Pretty much the same," I answered, knowing perfectly well that she could tell I was short-changing the truth. She shifted her sitting position back to a cross-legged one with her hands in her lap, palms up, fingers curled, and she tilted her head back, squinting at me with a skeptical look, mouth open, showing her two front teeth.

"What do you really do when you fly somewheres? You never tell me anything," she complained.

I'd been talking to her as if she were an eight-year-old, or how I thought I should talk to one, and clearly I was off the mark.

"Tell what you do when you go flying." She kept her head tilted back and hunched her shoulders for emphasis.

The war and the goings and comings of our planes had been in her consciousness for a long part of her short life, like the sun, moon, and stars, but also like sudden loud thunder claps in the rain or tree-tearing winds or the death of people. Even her questions about the likelihood of my survival were plain—she was precocious in a way that should not have surprised me. The mysteries of war were provocative.

Well, yes but maybe tomorrow. I was hardly up to it on a Merseburg day.

"Tell me," she said again.

So I did, although very carefully.

We went back to Munich two days after Merseburg, exchanging a violent box barrage for the work of well-educated tracking gunners, and if pressed, I would have to say that I hated the trackers only slightly less. On the bomb run Old Bird took a nasty splatter of 88 shrapnel left of the nose, letting in a bitter-cold torrent at full airspeed, which I covered with my flak suit and rode home feeling naked.

In the late afternoon Elizabeth came over to sit with me in the weedy grass to look at whatever was out there, composing herself in simple symmetry—elbows on knees, cheeks pressed firmly into the curving palms of both hands, tolerating the jumble of hair that fell across the corners of her eyes. Where'd we gone, she wondered, and

I told her that it had been to Munich, way down in the far corner of Germany—a long ways.

She didn't comment, still unused to being in the know, and I thought about the moments of truth when I'd told her what really happened when we went away with the big planes for so many hours at a time. I'd stressed simply, and with as little detail as possible, that we were breaking up places where the Germans made things to use against us and that that would end their ability to carry on the war. She seemed to find it all understandable, but beyond that she wanted my unwavering promise over again that I wouldn't get killed.

I suffered no combat fatigue during my tour, and in fact prospered. Lispeth may well have been salutary for the spirit—certainly she was a perfect antidote to flak poison; and if it was surcease from combat jitters that my ARMA needed, she'd pick a bouquet of weed flowers and present them to me with a solemn face usually tilted slightly leftward, lips parted in readiness for a word or two; or that being too passive on a really fine afternoon, she'd run full tilt against the wind out to a designated place and back, tangling expertly her flaxen hair in rhythmic whorls she knew I admired and flouncing her calico dress hip-high in complex configurations of Nature's design. She'd do this like a someday Olympian until the sweat trickled down her red cheeks and her usual seriousness would give way to shrieks of laughter.

One day I asked her "What do you do other times, you know, like when I've gone on a long flight or somewhere else, or when you're not around?"

"Oh, I help my mum in the garden or sew buttons or fix a rip in my dress, and read things in books. And a lot a times I drawr with those color pencils, but I can't get them near as good as yours. I made a picture of Gram in a hat once, and she gave me sixpence."

"Where are your brothers?" I asked next.

"They're not my brothers. They're cousins from Corby."

14

Lead Team

As far back as late June it had already been mentioned that we were being considered for lead-team evaluation and training. John had been with the 614th Squadron at its inception in Glasgow, Montana, before coming to Rapid City where he joined our crew. By this coincidence, our placement in the 401st Bomb Group reunited him with several old acquaintances who had risen in the hierarchy, and this may have drawn attention to us as a crew.

When this finally came before us, more or less as a proposal rather than a direct order, it created something of a strained situation. Lockhart was totally in favor, and so was I. Jardine had his reservations, and Ham did not seem to cast a vote. Of course Lockhart saw it as a multifaceted opportunity; almost immediate promotion and prestige and release from the long drudgery of formation flying, and I thought of it as a chance to increase my satisfaction with the job of being a navigator. Jardine reminded me, however, that it was the pilots' Air Force, and that my busywork would earn me no favors. The friction continued and gradually generated heat.

By the first of August, the decision was made to start flying us as squadron deputy-lead, and John made it clear that he wanted no part of the deal. I was sorry that it came to that, because I'd gotten comfortably used to his companionship in our penthouse in the B-17, and I was more than willing to keep it that way. The officers of our crew were thus rearranged. Russell Lockhart and I were joined by a bombardier named George Lewis, who must have been three or four years older than I was, and quite by chance he had the same number of mission credits as we did. He was mature, businesslike, and friendly, but only to a point. During our practice bombing at the Wash, I immediately found that he was a calm and very deliberate master of his trade.

We were also provided with a radar operator named Bill Strong, who was a flight officer with a blue bar insignia making him the equivalent of a warrant officer in the Army. As the radar, or "mickey," operator he had his office back in the radio room, and thus we met primarily at briefing.

While Lewis and I worked well in the air together and learned to have complete trust in each other, we never formed a close friendship, and I didn't even know where he lived in the squadron area. Although John began to fly with another crew, we still thought of him as one of us, and he continued to live in our Nissen.

When in August we began to fly squadron lead after a practice period as deputy, Porter was replaced in the right seat by a series of guest riders, persons of rank to give us command authority. They were various. On several letters of commendation that we received for textbook strikes under difficult circumstances, these illustrious personages were mentioned first, although they exercised their duties in the copilot seat while Russell and the autopilot did the flying. They did no navigating, no target identification, no bombsight synchronizing, but they gave us that difficult-to-define essence known as leadership. On three or four occasions it was our squadron commander, Major Eric de Jonckheere. He was a pleasant guy, and I liked him. So, while his contribution was somewhat intangible, he never caused a problem for us.

Porter was ultimately given a crew and finished his tour as a first pilot, or aircraft commander. But, as I've mentioned, we still lived together and thought of ourselves as "the crew."

Our crew reconstituted as a lead team, August 1944. *Back row, from left:* George Lewis, William Strong, Russell Lockhart, Porter Ham, and Otto Schlaegel. *Front:* Elno Pyles, Larry Million, Lloyd Null, and Robert Grilley.

A lead team, as it was constituted in the 401st Bomb Group, was the pilot, navigator, bombardier, and mickey operator. They practiced a good deal between missions, using a pickup copilot and dropping small marker bombs with ten-pound explosive charges on targets in a large shallow bay called the Wash, located just north of the bulge of East Anglia. The strikes were photographed, and the bombardier was graded for circular error, or CE. This was done at very high altitude to simulate real bomb runs. Lewis easily established one of the best CEs in the group, and soon Lockhart was assured of his promotion to captain and Lewis and I were promoted to first lieutenants on August 5.

Generally the group lead was rotated among the four squadrons, and one time when it was our turn, we drew a colonel for copilot. He was a staff officer from Wing headquarters and was the designated group leader. He was rather portly and seemed middle aged to us; but in retrospect, I doubt that he was even forty. A little metal ladder was brought out for him to use to climb up through the hatch, and we all glanced at each other with slight grins .

I can't remember for sure where the mission target was, but it was probably one of our tacticals, though I do remember the incident that marks the event. When we were about halfway to the IP and perfectly on course and on time, and I was enjoying a few peaceful moments with the plane steady as a house on autopilot, I began to notice a slight deviation to the right. It persisted, and I thought our gyro was going out. I called Lockhart and asked what was happening, whereupon he informed me that the colonel had set in a correction because we were getting off course. I was thunderstruck. Who did this guy think he was? The colonel came on the intercom and said that he had been this way before and recognized a checkpoint in the wrong place. I can't remember just how I expressed my exasperation, but I did sell him some peace of mind, that we had not, in fact, been off course. It surprised me that forty-eight years later at our group reunion, the incident was recalled by my crew members without prompting. Several of the guys even had him promoted to a brigadier.

15

Nienburg and Kettering

We began the work of August with a not-very-daunting tactical near Chartres. A German mechanized division remained obdurate longer than expected, and we were sent in to loosen them up. Things seemed to be going well when, with few shell bursts to be seen, one of our B-17s was hit badly and flamed instantly, almost taking the left member of its element with it in the disintegrating plunge. Several crewmen, as it turned out, were killed, but some were lucky enough to chute behind our lines and got back to base. You never knew—there weren't any real milk runs.

Then on the 5th, Nienburg, an industrial town in northern Germany, was presented to us by High Wycombe as a worthy target. I no longer have the log and briefing notes, but the image that my memory resolves is of a concentration of factory sheds in which aircraft parts made underground were assembled. Our effort was to be in necessary response to irrational antlike activity. The Enemy was continuing his burgeoning fighter production, but with a diminishing fuel supply. Merseburg and all the deep tanks had been hit hard, and who was to fly these well-made airplanes, the Hitler Youth, each with a total of fifty hours of solo? Our Little Friends had decimated their corps of professionals; but by then, no one could suppose that the Nazis were still capable of logic.

On a clear day, which it was, Holland was easy to navigate. At our altitude I was reminded of the wall maps in Vermeer, the cartography of sea and sand, the Dutch engineering genius had literally made a country out of ocean shallows and given them names.

We had attracted some scattered flak at coast-in but none of it threatening; and then for a while our ambiance was simply a fine summer day over the Ijesselmeer and polders on its eastern shore. There were times when reality was whatever my mind might make of it. The drone of the engines could fade and my fifty-pound equipage dissolved in thin air and bright sun. I could for long moments see the Netherlandish seascapes of the seventeenth century. Ruisdael was a truth the Nazi incursions had not replaced. But a few words over the intercom would draw me out.

"How long to the IP?" asks Russell.

"About a half hour."

"What's it called?"

"Vechta." Then I add, "We're on course to it now, and only have to alter five degrees there to start the run."

Afterward silence, a quiet time, when a senior crew no longer needs nervous chatter, drowsing in the bright light and hunched in the intense cold, each of us waiting with one eye open for something to happen.

We cross into Germany and soon are a few miles north of Meppen over the Ems river with Vechta almost in sight.

"IP in ten minutes, and then a ten-minute bomb run," I tell everyone.

Vechta slides under us, and we're in moderate flak, which becomes rather sharp as we alter a few degrees right to begin the run. Nienburg is on the quite-prominent Weser river, which has some helpful ox-bows rendering the target a sure thing, even with some attempts at camouflage. Lewis and I have the place well committed to memory from the P-38 photos. It's almost as if we've been there before. So with no false starts he locks on to some pretarget spots with the Norden. He glances up in momentary irritation when a harsh jolt of flak interrupts his concentration but continues with small corrections until course and rate are "killed" and the chosen spot, and indeed everything in the scope, is motionless. He then advances the crosshairs to the target and sets the index system in motion. Others in the squadron are staring at our open bomb bay waiting to salvo. The angular rate index mark reaches its preset point and automatically releases the bombs.

The flak still rages, and large black curling shapes threaten, but the ones we see are harmless; they've already sent out their little death missiles. The ones we haven't seen yet can kill any or all of us, and there appears to be no shortage. Each of us got up this morning and knew that some in the group might not come back to the shot of Irish or to chow or go on to continue their lives. A soldier, as distinct from a serviceman, wins the rest of his life or well-being in a lottery, and he's bought his ticket.

After bombs-away we make a long gradual turn to the left back to 285 degrees and begin our homeward trek. The mission planners have weighed the flak records and carefully decided that a left turn was better than a right. Nothing is allowed to chance except the unpreventable chaos of an air battle or a lost lead navigator.

We're back over the Ijesselmeer, and I'm mentally straying again. For a while I'll be unoccupied, and except for cold hands I'm not even uncomfortable. The large sea-lake fills a substantial part of my visual panorama. It must be quite smooth; there are no light-gray spume trails, no small ships to leave wakes. Did I ever tell you how long these missions are? This is only medium length, probably less than eight hours. I'm looking at nothing but water, and then there is something; a whitish-gray streak on the surface materializes in slow motion. At first I'm quietly puzzled; then I realize that it's a B-17 ditching; must be from the group ahead. I call it to our collective attention, but it's sliding back directly under us and only Million in the tail will be able to see it. It disappears; the location of the plane is too far away. We hope that the Germans pick up the crew; a stalag is very much better than the alternative.

At coast-out Russell backs off the throttles and further leans the mixture; we've made it again, and wonder what the cooks have done for us today. Beef stew will be just fine. We're coming over some scattered clouds, but nothing you could call weather, and at Great Yarmouth I tell Russ that 272 mag will do it and that we should be on the ground in twenty minutes. Lewis says something, the first I've heard from him since we coasted out. He points to three small flak holes in our Alcoa aluminum on the port side, but we can only find two corresponding ones on the other side; nothing much, since our skins are intact. Everyone on board can hear anything said on the intercom, so that sets off some light chatter about more flak holes. Our ground crew will have a little session with tinsnips and rivet guns, but nothing major.

We weren't posted by 1700, and since I'd been meaning to show Elizabeth the Kettering bookstore, I asked her mother to allow me the fun of taking her the next morning, and both of them were pleased.

The rattling coal gas–burning bus was exceptionally slow, and every design feature that could make seats uncomfortable had been incorporated, so it was not at all difficult to provoke two already dyspeptic looking women who had been suffering the seats and exhaust fumes all the way from Oundle, with fourteen more miles to go to Kettering, into wordless criticism of Liz and me—she for her insouciant manner, feet up on the seat back in front of her nudging one of the hats, and me for permitting it. I returned their unhappy glances with a smile that admitted no offense and even tipped my cap ever so slightly. Liz paid them not the least bit of recognition and kept her gaze on views of the countryside.

She was surprisingly familiar with turns in the road and pointed out a farm owned, or at least lived on, by her mother's cousin, which launched her into a brief narrative about how they had some red pigs there and a goat that she had once sat on when she was considerably younger. They'd gotten milk from the goat, but it had a funny taste, and, she added, with a nose-wrinkling squint that it was not easy to persuade her to try it again.

The stone buildings were similar in style and construction to Yokehill Farm, appearing to be of the same period, that is, the same century, although less impressive in scale. I'd paused to look at them several times while biking and had put them on my mental list for drawing.

About a mile into Kettering on a prominent street near the railroad station, which together with the bookshop was my usual purpose for using the bus, we got off. Lispeth who was well rested and feeling the need of some athletic effort, jumped well out toward the curb without touching the three steps. She was good at that sort of thing but had certainly overestimated her levitating powers, and she came down on hands, knees, and slippers with more weight than I'd guessed she totaled—five and a half stone and maybe a little more. I stood motionless for five seconds and leaped down myself to assess the damage. She rolled to her left, and I could see that her face, including mouth and nose, had probably not reached the ground. There were abrasions leaking some blood serum from her knees and scratches on her palms. She was beginning to huff a bit, but, all told, doing pretty well. The lady driver stepped down, hugged her up, and kissed her.

"You all right, love?"

I mopped her with my clean handkerchief and sat her on the curb until I was sure we had no catastrophe on our hands. The tears streamed liberally from her eyes and nose, but she was far too proud to cry.

It was about eleven-thirty, and things were quite a bit better than the first moments off the bus could have promised. We were sitting in a green park with a fish-and-chips stand fifty feet away. Her dress had a small knick in its hem, and her slipper a scratch that could be blackened.

In a few more minutes she was ready for some fish and chips and a strawberry pop, and to get on with what we came for.

The proprietress of the bookshop was named Mrs. J. Poole. Her husband had been a bibliophile since his youth and, with a small legacy, had bought the rather picturesque-looking place stocked with this and that. He decided early on that in Kettering used copies in good condition moved and were more readily accessible than new stock; at least for him they were. Mrs. Poole was a nearly perfect helpmate. She was two or three years older, with no children to demand a portion of her attention, so when the Germans had to be taken seriously, Mr. James was hustled off to do his part, and with great good fortune he found an assignment in an army tech manual office in London. How did I know? His wife was loquacious to a point one seldom encounters.

So she carried on his growing used-goods direction with enthusiasm. Their location near the railroad station and the park was an undoubted advantage; and during the war, things were bought and sold cheap. Who would pay what books were worth when the staples of life were scarce? One does what she can. I was a lucky find: a university degree in the liberal arts and, best of all, an American flying officer with money in his pockets and a taste for English literature and fine-quality books of art reproductions. She'd not encounter such patrons browsing her offerings every day or fortnight.

Elizabeth was for her a delight, and she gave her an unmerciful squeeze. Luckily Liz had made a quick recovery and was already in a receptive mood, which the smiling proprietress took as a compliment. So when Mrs. Poole had finished her effusive greeting, I mopped the still-oozing knees, and we were ready for business. Liz, unfamiliar with a place of such specialization, stood looking at the tables and shelves of books that varied greatly in size, color, and cover design, and one could suppose that she might even be judging their age and condition. Perhaps I'd again, as I had in other situations, underestimated her and had expected her to make her rounds quickly handling almost everything that could be lifted from the tables or pulled down from the shelves. More likely she was simply deciding on a manner of expression for her usual boldness. Mrs. Poole smiled at her again and indicated that it was time to go to work. Elizabeth squinted at her in return.

Standing behind her skylighted sales table, she came to the point without further overtures. "Lieutenant, I do clearly remember that you asked me to keep an eye out for a good *Alice,* and now I've a notion why. You'll find it hard to credit such luck, but just yesterday in the late afternoon, a beautiful, exceptionally well-annotated copy came in; a most excellent publication in flawless condition; not a mark or scratch on the substantial jacket, and the Tenniel illustrations are clear on ivory-colored, glossy coated paper. As you know, James, my husband, is in the army and works in a technical manual office in London, which gives him occasional chances to find things in shops there for our trade, and this is just such a pick of good fortune."

With that descriptive promise she pulled the obviously splendid copy from a shelf under her table and placed it squarely before me. Short of a detailed perusal it was entirely as represented, and I bought it straight away for eighteen shillings.

"Of course, we'll have it. Won't we, Hon?"

Elizabeth showed her affirmation by standing firmly up against me and nuzzling her face under my arm with a nod now and then.

Mrs. Poole smiled and even winked. "You'll no doubt remember asking for a good copy of *Wuthering Heights,* and here's a clean one with some quite fine illustrations. They're rather plentiful so I'm only asking seven shillings; reasonable, I think."

Liz affirmed with an increase in pressure on my hand and an up-and-down movement on her toes, that we'd have that one, too.

The books were tied up with wide green ribbons and deposited in the cloth bag that Liz's mom had sent, there being no paper for such purposes. I added a well-kept copy of the 1938 Royal Watercolor Society catalog to our purchase and let Elizabeth pick out some fresh colored pencils and a thick drawing pad.

It was still quite early, and I seem to remember that we were unable to pass a shop of cheap knick-knacks and jewelry without lingering and finally entering. First an engraved brass bracelet trimmed with artificial jade could not be left. Then there were thin 14k-gold rings with which size presented no problem unless you were an exceptionally fat lady. Finally there was the necklace so delicate that one had to look closely to see it. Lispeth clasped the jewels in her hand, tightly to her cheek, making her eyes seem even bluer. There must have been other things, but not that time.

A little further along we came to a rose garden that required our admiration and much comparative sniffing, with differing opinions, and, of course, the unqualified declaration that England—especially Northhamptonshire—was the true land of roses, to which Liz nodded while the wind blew her hair in a variety of tangles.

It's likely that we had more strawberry pop with fish and chips and something sweet. Although the English had learned to accept sugarless substitutes, which did not satisfy my American palate, Liz seems to have drawn little distinction between Milky Way bars and the strange flavors concocted for wartime British desserts.

Our ride back to the Yokehill Farm road would not have coincided with the return of the ladies to Oundle, and I doubt that anyone else would have complained about Elizabeth's immodest posture with her feet up on the seat in front of her. Those who noticed her at all usually smiled and made glib remarks

When the bus stopped at our road, Liz, well able to profit by experience, would have needed no reminder to disembark in a proper way in spite of her athletic urges, and she quite likely would have given me a knowing smile.

Then, she would have gotten out of her slippers for the walk back to the farm, but the bus ride having lulled her, would also have recharged her battery, so, not being able to further suppress herself, she would have scampered in the long grass between the hedge and the road, looking, at a distance, like a large windblown butterfly.

One might ask how I was able to briefly come and go across the boundaries of our base at times when my services were not scheduled. The answer is somewhat provisional and at variance with certain other military commands. In the first place, there were no fences, only gates at the main road entrances where identification might be required. Then, too, there was the rather aristocratic system involving a distinction between officers and enlisted men, which implied quite improbably that officers might be expected to act in a more responsible way. At Deenethorpe junior officers could pass these not very imposing barriers by a flash of our Adjutant General Office pass; but the admonition was always present in our minds that not being there for duty was a serious offense subject to more than a reprimand.

The 613th was not posted for the next day, quite likely by squadron rotation, so Porter and I, as we occasionally did, set out after chow for a stroll to the Benefield pub to quaff "bitter" ale. It's easy to conjecture some of our talk. Marion was in college as an English lit major and would be a teacher, so her academic adventures came through as a lively account in her letters, and Porter, with possessive pride, often gave me an extensive report. Other topics, of course, included airplanes and what we intended to do after the duration-plus.

An evening in The Hawk and the Grouse was very much like entering into a movie and participating. The regulars, the villagers and farmers, treated us with a deference that probably was not accorded by elders to their juniors, although there were times when loud Americans wore out their welcome before closing time. I enjoyed the native's use of preradio country English, an older variant on our mutual tongue that seemed to have value worth collecting for its own sake.

At the latitude of our location, 52 degrees north, there would be a chill at night even in midsummer, and our leather jackets over woolen shirts were just right. We would walk at halfpast midnight, hands in pockets, over the road back to our Nissen in a glowing darkness, the trees silhouetted against a sky of blurred stars.

By 0100 we were in the sack, early by comparison with the roisters among us. John, returning at 0200, was usually able to reduce his recitations to a mumble, and I, only lifting an eyelid, might exchange a few muttered words with him. Lockhart, already snoring in deep sleep, would not have noticed any of this. He did like his sack time, which certainly contributed to his mental and physical well-being as a tireless pilot.

On August 8 we dropped a number of 250-pounders on a tactical near Hautmesnil in France. I remember very little about it except that we gave the Germans quite a pasting with very little in return. A few more of those cost-free bomb runs and those in charge would be adding to our tour number; but you couldn't honestly complain if they did. Certainly a tactical didn't equate with Merseburg or Leipzig. Theoretically it would all balance out with odds a little better than Russian roulette.

16

Peenemünde

The meaning of the word *spectacular* has been diminished by careless use, so I should find a more appropriate word to describe our twenty-first mission—possibly *beautiful*—flown on the 25th of August. It was to Peenemünde, the V2 rocket research and production facility located on the Baltic coast north of Berlin. Visually it provided the ultimate. Things that had been partially realized during some of our previous missions converged and came into sharp focus, and I was able to see the full depth and sweep of a magnificent aerial panorama.

From coast-out at Lowestoft we took up a heading of about 50 degrees, which would carry us well clear of the Dutch and German Frisian Islands where flak could be regularly expected. Visibility was excellent to begin with, but at a point about midway across the North Sea an unusual wall of clouds appeared at a distance across our course. It was unusual in that it seemed, as we approached, to present a flat vertical surface that extended from sea level to a height far above our altitude, which was probably at the time 24,000 feet, and it ran from the northern to the southern horizons. There was no possibility of safely flying a formation of B-17s into such a dense cloud mass, so the group commander calmly ordered us to go up. Up, up. The B-17 could do it. It was an indomitable war horse. At 28,000 feet the summits were still lofty and dazzling as the easterly sunlight slanted down across them. At 29,000 feet we were getting close to the wall, but I could not say with certainty how near it was. At this proximity it still maintained its smooth vertical form. Was it ten miles? Hard to say, but it seemed that we would have to change course to have a longer run to get over it. The group commander was mum. Perhaps this was the kind of thing that we needed him for. By this time I was a pretty experienced navigator, but I knew nothing about the upper-level performance capabilities of this wonderful flying machine, especially at gross load and in formation. I had never been this high before, and neither had Russell. At 30,000 feet the other ships were beginning to drift here and there a bit. We had gone another ten miles and still the wall seemed well out in front of us. Up, up. The rate-of-climb needle wavered slightly at 100 feet per minute.

At this point I began to notice how intensely cold it was getting. My gloves were inadequate, and my fingers were beginning to feel numb, but I still had control of them. I squeezed my oxygen tube to crunch the ice, and had had to detach it momentarily to shake out the pieces, but in the process I had averted my eyes for only a minute at the most, and when I returned my gaze to this awesome white phenomenon, I could see some irregular patches on its wall. They began to look more like clouds, and the summits seemed wispy in the fierce sunlight.

At 31,500 feet we were there, and about to cross over. I glanced sideward to my left down along the gauzy west side of the wall from my perch in the nose bowl, down into the deep shadow, down to the nearly black surface of the sea, and I felt an instant of dread and yet exhilaration. Never had I been so high, and never before had I been able to see it in this perspective. Then we were skimming through the diaphanous material of the summits. Contrails had begun to form earlier, but because of our privileged position our visibility was not hampered.

My air plot was still intact, and I'd been able to get Gee fixes until we were quite close to the cloud wall. I had managed to divert my attention from my fascination with it long enough occasionally to calculate our changing true airspeed and ground speed—more precisely, our sea speed—so fortunately I knew where all of this was taking place.

We must certainly have reached the jet stream at this altitude, and by conjecture I added another twenty knots to the west wind that metro had granted us at 24,000 feet. The cloud mountain range was less than forty miles wide at the top, and in about seven minutes we were beginning to let down. The blinding-white east slopes seemed more irregular, and there were a few separate cloudlets in the otherwise clear air.

I hated to see us throw away all that altitude. We'd surely have to climb back over the thing again going home, and by afternoon it might well be higher, but with our bombs gone and a lighter fuel load we could make it. Or could we? This was starting to look like a ten-hour airplane ride; but we were on autopilot with a minimum fuel burn, so unless we got flak in the gas tanks we'd be okay. Some of the poor stiffs flying formation might have to go to Sweden and sit out the rest of the duration-plus. However, speculation was of no use here; we had to get back down to a bombing altitude of 24,000 feet. Our target was small and required some accurate synchronizing and a closely hugged-up formation. If we tried it from 31,000 feet we'd be way out of the ballpark, and could just as well have stayed home in the sack.

Abruptly we came out over the eastern edge of the cloud mountain in superclear air, and, almost to my surprise, I found that we were virtually on course over the Schleswig-Holstein peninsula just south of Flensburg. But it was hard to believe what lay spread out before me: a view from Valhalla. Could Odin himself have seen it like this?

Denmark, nearly all of it, could be scanned at a glance, even the northern tip dimmed only slightly in a transparent silver haze; and across the Kattegat was Sweden, up to its shimmering lake-strewn middle. The Danish islands over to Copenhagen and beyond seemed like a cartographer's graphic construction. And down over the edge of the world to the right lay all of Germany.

We had taken off at 0621 hours and now were at Flensburg at 0922. Our course would continue for a hundred miles to Vordingborg, southwest of Copenhagen, where we would alter to a direct easterly heading to the southern tip of Bornholm, the last of the Danish islands, which lay well out into the dark-blue Baltic about twenty-five miles southeast of Sweden.

Even before reaching Flensburg we had been using a very low power setting and had floated down to 27,000 feet. At about ten miles short of our geographic point of turn, to the south at Bornholm, we began our gradual swing to a heading of 180 degrees. A formation requires a long turning radius, and if you are a little behind time you can pick up a few minutes by cutting it slightly shorter. In effect, we were making a huge U-turn to begin our bomb run. The coordinates for our initial point were 54°40′ N and 15° E—simply a spot in the Baltic, nothing but a white cap, a new experience for me as well as for Lewis.

At 1056 we had passed the invisible IP and were established on a bomb run with a heading of 262 degrees. At a point about forty-five miles from the target, we were down to our assigned bombing altitude of 24,000 feet, which was lower than usual, but with such a small and valuable target, every foot of circular error would be costly. Our 613th squadron box was tightening up nicely, with no bumps. It would be a good bomb pattern. Of course all of us up front had a perfect view of Peenemünde in the clear air. It lay at the tip of a small peninsula on an island northwest of the Oder river estuary; however, synchronizing the Norden in advance was impossible. In our usual procedure, Lewis could correct course and establish angular rate using a ground object under our flight path and advance the sight markers to the target later for refinement before the bomb release. It was time for Bill Strong to get into the act.

We had a rather stiff head wind, so our sea speed was little more than 178, giving us a bomb run, from the time we rolled out on our heading, of nearly thirteen minutes. At 1102 Strong announced that we were at the twenty-five-mile range, so Lewis could start programming that in for later refinement. In another three minutes he was able to get the target into his sight, and he worked with the same calm detachment that he showed practicing at the Wash.

The enemy's reception committee did not use a box barrage; rather, they used remarkably sharp tracking flak, and several of their earlier shots seemed to be aimed personally at us. Why not? It's logical; hit the lead and see if the deputy has things under control. *Crack! Crack!* I could feel the concussive pressure of them.

At 1109 Lewis called bombs-away in his laconic manner, quite oblivious of the flak, and leaned way out past the Norden to watch the bomb strike.

"Okay, " He commented. "Looks okay." It was as if he were judging a good golf shot.

Of course the strike was photographed, and I was sure that his CE would measure out great. Our formation was tight with no bobbing or weaving, and Lewis was truly a businessman, or maybe instead a fine artist playing a demanding instrument.

We turned 30 degrees to the right and in three or four minutes were out of the flak. Our four fans were all roaring at their usual decibel levels, and no gas was spraying out. Nobody reported losing any blood, and no vital equipment had been trashed, but it would be a draftier and colder ride home. Narrow icy shafts of wind shot back from three or four one-inch-sized holes in the Plexiglas just to the right of the nose bowl, and there were several under my station with corresponding exit holes in the ceiling:ventilation at a 150-mile-an-hour indicated airspeed at forty degrees below zero. This, of course, was not unusual, but nothing like our ripping at Hamburg or Berlin or at the flak capital, Merseburg, but still, sharp-tracking flak by experts was eerie.

Soon after our turn, Million reported that two planes from the 615th box far off to our right were dropping back. Maybe they had wounded that would not last all the way to England, or maybe they were bleeding gas or had lost an engine or two. Sweden was a hundred

miles across the Baltic, and a careful expenditure of altitude might get
them there.

Our course took us over a large irregularly shaped island called
Rugen. There was no flak there, no priority. We coasted out at 1121,
exactly five hours from takeoff, and it was beginning to look like we
might have to make another big climb. Already there was weather
down to the surface of the sea ahead. But the tops seemed to be
broken into tall columns, and it might be that we could slip between
some of them. They had drifted about seventy miles east of their earlier position, and there was a noticeable cleft in the wall a little south
of our flight plan course. We headed for that and slithered through
at 26,000 feet. The cloud tops were frothy and the passage had
broadened to cover the whole Schleswig-Holstein portion of the big
peninsula.

At 1257 we were clear of the clouds and could begin our gradual
letdown. It was about 450 miles home, and with our descent against
a strong headwind with a modest power setting, we could expect to
average about 160 miles per hour. Three hours would do it, and I
gave us an ETA of four o'clock, or 1600 in the log. Actually, I was allowing for a little slippage, time in the pattern and such.

At 12,000 feet over the North Sea, within two hundred miles of
East Anglia, Lewis and I probably both took off our masks. Our flak
suits would have come off much earlier. He would have immediately
lit a cigarette but would probably have had little to say. He might
have been relieved but taciturn. I missed Jardine's sometimes sharp
humor; it always took some weight off the long hours.

We touched down at Deenethorpe at 1556, after nine hours and
thirty-five minutes in the air, and were met at the hardstand to be
hauled immediately to interrogation. They paused long enough for
the photo technician to grab the strike photo negative sheets and
then we, the up-front crew, were off in a hurry. When we arrived, I
had to make a phone call to Wing, which always surprised me. They
wanted a verbal synopsis from a direct source. You'd think they'd want
it from the right-seat brass, our designated command authority; but
no, they wanted it from someone with it all written down, someone

Interrogation, August 1944. *From left:* Elno Pyles, George Lewis, Russell Lockhart, Robert Grilley, unidentified interrogation officer, Porter Ham, and William Strong.

who had looked at the maps and made the measurements and recorded the times and events.

When I got back, our gunslingers were drifting in, and our little seminar was about to begin. The youngish middle-aged intelligence officer gathered us around his table, and the gorgeous Red Cross girl saw to it that a steaming pot of coffee with a can of Carnation milk and a pan of cake with maple fudge frosting were in the middle. Then she tactfully withdrew so as not to interfere. Pity, it had been a visually splendid day, and she certainly capped it.

17

Berlin II

After Peenemünde, it looked as if we might slip through the rest of August unscathed and I was in a languorous mood. What I'd seen of Germany seemed sufficient to last for quite a while, although summer has always been the best time to make war, so maybe a tactical or two might well be used to round out a memorable season.

But the little left of August brought us to our boots very early one morning, so early that nothing good could come of it, and when the curtain was drawn aside, it was Berlin, my mission twenty-two. The noise was to be expected, and Colonel Bowman stood there with a patient look on his handsome face. Finally he raised his hand just a bit to ask for quiet and it was granted, except that the bombardier's fox terrier barked and set us back a few happy seconds. People were always ready to lighten up for such moments, so the dog's comment was considered germane, and we hoped that he would make another. But Bowman, with a tolerant grin, reminded us that we really had to get back to the purpose of our gathering.

"Gentlemen," he began, "today we are going to give the Berliners the first installment on a double whammy." The choice of words sounded a bit odd from such a formal man. "Today the Eighth is going to put a thousand planes over Berlin, and tonight the RAF will do the same. You will use 500-pounders, eight per ship, and drop them by intervalometer. This will be a maximum effort, and it's hoped that it will help the enemy to take stock of his hopeless position. Our P-51s will be out on seek-and-destroy missions, trying to make your day a little less exciting. Good luck."

Goddamn, we were back to that eye-for-an-eye stuff. How many civilians would our 613th, with Lewis at the bombsight, kill today? I hoped from my heart that they'd gotten all their skinny little kids out of town. Hammering and burning cities did not work against the English. Why was it expected to work against Europe's most disciplined, bull-headed, people?

There would be exceptions of course, but Northhamptonshire's warm southwest August wind normally favored runway two-three for takeoffs. It was so long and smooth, in fact, that it was often the runway of choice even with a mild crosswind at gross load. Straight, at full throttle after liftoff and up out of ground effect—our war for the day begun—we would cross the boundary road and a rocky field, then pass over my beloved Landscape; and after a mile with remarkable regularity, begin our long climbing turn to the left using the Yokehill Farm house as an ample distanced point of radius, the wing tip seeming to point at it during the passage around a half-circle, setting us on our compass heading of 50 degrees in line for the formation radio splasher at Kings Lynn.

On this, or any such similar morning, Elizabeth must have awakened listening to us while clutching her knees tightly to her chin until the roar of the great birds had died away and she could hear the hall clock ticking. There would have been a quickening of her heart during those many long minutes, but then the deep relieving sleep of childhood would return for a few hours until the normal sounds of the farm's own early morning would awaken her to a long, loosely arranged day.

With minor course changes we used nearly the same route in and out as we had in June. The whole area was so saturated with flak positions that the most important decision was how to get in and out over the shortest land distance—that is, after we'd passed the relative emptiness of the North Sea, which that day was a deep gray-blue. We coasted in at Heide, or just south of it, on the Schleswig-Holstein peninsula, and before we reached Neumünster we were treated to the heartwarming sight of 51s hell-bent for some rapidly scattering Me-110s. There were two or three more flights of FW-190s, and altogether the opposition was impressive, but the Mustangs did make things tolerable. Of course they steered clear of the barrages, and so did the German fighters, and we took the expected pounding from the 88s and 105s.

My thoughts on the bomb run were much the same as they had been before. In the barrage my solipsism was thin as a soap bubble. I did have these moments, but they usually didn't last very long, not much longer than the cordite smell.

18

Good-bye, Elizabeth

After Berlin I had one of those luxurious rows of free days, six of them, as it turned out, with a trifling of practice on two of the mornings. It was late summer with a hint of fall in the air; cloudy mostly, but still good outdoor weather. I'd accumulated a variety of drawings in my little gray linen-covered portfolio and was spending some afternoon time reading to Liz. We'd gotten through *Alice,* where she'd memorized "You Are Old Father William" so we could recite it in unison, until she'd break into snorts and gasps of laughter. But on the afternoon when we began *Through the Looking Glass,* I could see that she was somewhat preoccupied, so when I previewed "Jabberwocky" and failed to arouse a peal of high-pitched mirth, I was sure that something had interceded, and I asked if she was sick.

"No, but my mum's going to take me to stay in Kettering with Annie so's I can go to school there," she moaned. "And I don't like her; she scolds me all the time."

"But isn't that where you went before?"

"No, to Benefield, but I always came home after."

"Well maybe the Benefield school's just for younger kids, and Kettering's too far to take the bus. Did you tell your mom why you don't like Annie?"

She looked at me with impatience. "Yes, and she just says it's okay an' that Annie really likes me and'll make nice things for me. But I don't want to stay with her."

She'd reached a state where reason hadn't the slightest appeal and assumed a fixed frown. I made a brief effort to redirect her attention to "Jabberwocky," but her mood would not be lightened until, at our arrival at the kitchen door, her mom invited me in for tea, whereupon the frown was transformed into a merely pensive look. She sat down across the big square table from me and consciously struck a well-practiced pose, saying, in effect, just look what you'll be missing.

Time pauses for a moment, and I consider her implied admonition. She's motionless, gazing at me as if it's possible for her to extend that moment at will.

The right side of her face is illuminated by a single tall window that penetrates the thick stone wall, and cool light reflecting from a blue and pink oilcloth on the table gives form to the left side of her chin and cheek with its attenuated lavender glow.

Again her mom is speaking, probably just an immediate repetition. My review of Elizabeth's appearance has taken only the moment. "With our Kettering arrangement you'll be happy as a lark in no time at all, won't you, love?"

Liz, half listening, nods slowly two or three times and sticks out her upper lip. She scans the cover of *Alice,* which lies centered on the table in front of her, and manipulates the lower right corner of the dust jacket. "Can't you finish the *Looking Glass* part for me? Sometime—I mean. Can't you?" The *Can't you?* requires a deep breath, and it issues with a sighing sound.

Her mom answers for me. "Maybe sometime, love, but the lieutenant has lots of flying to do, and you know you'll be going to Annie's the day after tomorrow."

Time continues unmeasured. I sip my tea, now grown cold, and make a reply, but to whom I'm not sure.

Her mom continues to speak, clunking her cup down in the saucer. "Annie'll be glad to have her there for a while. She likes to sew, and she'll make some proper things for our Liz."

I look at the child's drawings pinned to the wall on both sides of a large oak breakfront. Lispeth has not shown them to me, and I can't quite gauge the drawing proficiency, but her use of color is right and applied without hesitation. I've seen other children's drawings, although if I think of it, it's been some time ago. These might really be quite good for her age, but then I'm a biased judge.

The clouds have thickened and the light has diminished considerably, although it's still early afternoon. It'll probably rain soon. Liz has been staring round-eyed at me, but she glances down and drops her left hand, with a smack, to help the other one find the title page of *Through the Looking Glass*. "Can't you read it to me?" she asks without the faintest hope that I'll be able to.

The extended moment passed and the rain started—first a few drops on the lower panes, then heavily, all the way to the top of the window. I stood up and thanked her mom for asking me in and told Liz I was sure she'd love school in Kettering, that it would be fun to have lots of kids to play with. Then a simple good-bye would have to do. She squinted at me and snuffed her pink wet nose, flattening it with the back of her hand. If she said anything more, it was lost in the sound of the rain blown against the window.

At 1700 we were posted for a mission the next morning.

19

Ludwigshafen

Every soldier knows it can happen, and at times he wonders what it could be like—the flash, the pain and moment of bitter regret— light darkening into invisible gray, and then a forever-lasting silence. It's to be expected in the great barrages at Berlin or Merseburg, but the Germans have enough going on here too to keep their tracking guns well warmed. We've just trampled on the I. G. Farben Chemical Works in Ludwigshafen. It's midday September 3; mission twenty-three.

We've made a thirty-mile bomb run from the southwest through surprisingly scattered flak, and each of our dozen birds has dropped nine 500-pounders and turned over the Rhine on a long curving course downstream which is in fact northward toward Worms. The river is crowded with barges, and I suspect that many of them have one or more batteries of four heavies that they can bring to bear. I've caught sight of gun flashes, and very soon we'll know how well schooled their gunners are. Complex optical instruments and trig tables allow them to triangulate our altitude and angular speed and even the degree of our turn. They know the muzzle velocity of their shells and their deceleration rate; hence the trajectory and time it will take for them to overtake and meet us at an exact point in space. Their fuses have been timed for that special moment. The only things the gunners can't know on their first shots are the vagaries of the deflecting winds through which the shells must pass. Twenty-six thousand feet up and several miles' lead is a hell of a lot of space. They can mess up, and more often than not they do, or they'd have won the war by now. Jardine used to say, "It's the luck of the pot shot, and it depends on whose luck you're talking about."

The first four 88s burst about a hundred yards ahead of us—four more from another battery explode a bit to their left, fired a second after the first ones had left their guns. Russell turns back to a straight run; we can take some evasive action with our bombs gone, but not much for the sake of protective order in the formation. They've fired again; many are firing now. A shell has passed through the middle of our right wing almost unnoticed, seemingly soundless in the ambient noise until the explosion occurs a fraction of a second later at a point thirty feet above and out a like distance from the right gun port. It rakes the plane with several hundred pieces of shrapnel ranging in size from a broken pencil tip to jagged fragments an inch or more in length. None of us is hit, Lord of mercy, but Death is still deciding what to do about us. A tall geyser of fuel is instantly transformed into a vapor cloud while mixing with the hot exhaust gases from the number-three engine—this could be that ultimate moment, but it isn't. Nature is indecisive. One would have expected it much sooner.

Russ doesn't wait for the chemistry of the instant. He chops the throttle and pulls the mixture, killing engine three; and all within the same moment, he feathers the prop, stopping its rotation, which otherwise would drive the remaining hot exhaust into the ready-to-blow air fuel mixture.

"Grilley," Russ bellows, "exactly where the hell are we, and how far to coast-out?"

Well, I do have my pencil on our German place in spite of what's happening. "Worms, seventeen miles down-river, which means north. You should be turning to a heading of 270 degrees by now. We're about 300 from Calais, but that's not the formation's course.

They'll coast out at Abbeville. It's almost the same land distance, but twice as far over water."

So—in a minute or two Russ, Pyles, and I have done some high-altitude math—our takeoff gross weight had been about 65,000 pounds. Of that we've relieved ourselves of 4,500 pounds of bombs—burned more than 7,000 pounds of fuel at six pounds per gallon getting here, and about 900 pounds have been lost from the bulls-eye tank. This has lightened us considerably, and it will be downhill, so to speak, all the way home. But while the others with their four engines throttled back are conserving fuel, Russell has to advance the power settings on his remaining three to what amounts to a climb consumption.

Pyles comes on the line. "We're gulping over 180 gallons an hour—it won't last—we don't even have 700 gallons left, and I'm not sure about any of the right-side tanks and lines. The small flak pieces have punched some holes that aren't sealing. We could get down to 120 an hour if we cut the power to twenty-six inches and lean them good, but we'd sure settle out."

"Well, if we don't," I cut in, "we'll end up someplace that the Germans still own, or in the drink."

"We'll do it," says Russell. "What do we have guns for?"

"Do what besides dropping out?" I ask. "Go straight to the Pas de Calais on a letdown?"

"Okay with you, sir?" Russell mumbles to our silent and almost forgotten guest-command copilot.

"Yeah, okay, sure. We have to do something." What could the poor guy say?

Communications made with our squadron, we reduce power and begin our long descent, and in two or three minutes the deputy has taken our place. Our letdown will be at 200 feet a minute for an hour before leveling at 12,000 feet on a heading of 290 degrees to bring us out just south of Dunkirk. I stand with my head up in the astrodome as far as my helmet allows and watch the formation pass slowly over us. The relative motion shows them to be climbing away to our left until they become a flight of model B-17s, then formless

131

and finally gone. After I get back to business, I glance again through my side window, but they're truly gone; we're alone eighty miles inside the German Rhineland, with occupied Luxembourg and most of Belgium to cross. Every eye is scanning for dark hostile spots against the sky.

Some scattered and then broken clouds begin to form below us at from 10,000 to 15,000 feet. Nature is showing us her kind side again. If aggressive dark things appear, we can get down into the upper cloud layers quickly. But none come, and our descent path continues. A time-distance check shows our ground speed to be 140, in a little less than thirty minutes we're over Luxembourg, but still we might stray over some railroad flak batteries. The Germans are still in charge here.

By the time we've gotten down among the scattered clouds, we're over the Belgian Ardennes region, and our course must be taking us near Bastogne (still unknown to us and to world news). It's been quiet for awhile since we left the formation. Russell says something to Pyles, but inaudible to me, and it's answered so briefly that it seems of no importance. Now after we've passed the Ardennes, I feel a small thrill-chill when I note Yvoir directly ahead through a large break in the clouds. It was a tactical target we'd flown back in mid-August, and our little tour group would surely find it of interest, so I call it to their attention.

Our continuing letdown takes us in and out of the clouds for the rest of the way to coast-out. Russ also knows of the RAF emergency field in Kent, and I give him a heading to it. My Gee fixes are coming in crisp, and there'll be no problem finding the place. The IFF (Indicator, Friend or Foe) is switched on. How very English for a little coded transmitter that can tell our people not to shoot at us.

Halfway across the Channel we let down through the clouds, which are thickening and becoming a dark overcast. The water is slate color and the foam caps only a shade lighter, but the cliffs are indeed white, as their postcards promise (I certainly should buy one to send home), and the green Kentish fields would surely by now be sporting their early fall flowers.

It only takes sixteen minutes to cross the Channel, and the engines are running smoothly enough, but the slate-colored water makes me uneasy, as it always does when it's that hue. Soon we're over the deep green of fields and woods, and a Gee line of position has us on final approach with a few dollops in the tanks. After we've landed, a Limey sergeant in a small truck leads us to parking, where engine number four fumes dry and gives a little kick before we get entirely squared around.

Each of us, as we get our boots on the ground, runs over as quickly as possible to see our mark of destiny. The 88 hole doesn't look as large as I'd expected it to, but it's nonetheless pretty impressive.

"Damned lucky, sir," says the RAF man to Russell. "Damned lucky, you were."

Russ scratches his slightly English-looking aquiline nose and agrees, "You damned betcha." Then he gives his .45 automatic to Null and tells him to guard the plane until it's officially signed off. "And don't let anybody get near that Goddamned mickey set."

After a few questions and forms to be signed, they give us each a shot of unnamed scotch and send us home in a well-worn C-47, which they call a Dakota. A smiling sergeant, somewhat older than any of us, is our pilot, and although he's courteous it's plain that he considers RAF sergeant pilots an easy match for U.S. first lieutenants, and who could argue with that. Death by black-night collision is just as fiery as it is by 88s, and somewhat more of an occult experience.

We get back to Deenethorpe even before expected and have a crackerjack of an interrogation. Our judgment and performance is examined in what seems to me to be surprising detail, and it's not found wanting. It's always nice when the functionaries say that you've done it right. Occasionally I still smart from an early mistake I felt had been harshly judged.

Even Eric de Jonckheere comes by to complement us for saving a well-appointed mickey-equipped plane, adding that they cost the

Air Force a real bundle. He fails to note that it cost more to fully train a bomber crew than to build a machine; and, above that incomparably, to save all nine of our lives is surely in a class by itself. As mentioned, we've gotten back early and after a dose of Irish they hardly have to warm up the chow, beef stew; a little stringy, but still good.

Unaccountably, after such a demanding way to spend a large part of the day, I didn't feel gone. Combat flying at age twenty-three must have enlarged the adrenals. My ARMA was delighted to be back. Certainly something seemed to have been proven. Although, as we've agreed, there are no milk runs, we may have had our crisis; no more direct hits. Look at all those coincidences—an 88 right through the worst possible place, but we were on the way out with our bombs gone, and the fuel geyser that didn't flame when anyone's common sense should have expected it to. For all of that, we could have blown up at any time on the way back; empty tanks wet with fuel fumes are primed with a lethal mixture. And then, too, we weren't caught by German thugs while we were alone miles behind our protective formation—all one hell of a good omen. Someday we'd finish clean and go home to grow old slowly and tell of the deeds of our youth, like Henry's men from the field of Agincourt. So quite properly I should have been down at the Benefield pub, The Hawk and the Grouse, at the moment drinking bitters, pint after pint after pint. I surely wouldn't be posted for the next day.

It was about four in the afternoon, or 1600 hours, if you like it that way; remember the two hour daylight time though, so it would have only been the middle of the real afternoon; they surely wouldn't have to get us up so early for this kind of schedule. The clouds were unbroken and bore a September expression. Rain? In all of England who could know, although I'm sure the city folk would have had their big umbrellas in hand.

I wasn't at The Hawk and the Grouse, though, or at the officer's club celebrating one more misfire of fate. I was sitting in a leg-extended sprawl against the oak with my multipurpose sheepskin jacket rolled as a cushion. The massive tree branched widely and provided all but heavy rain protection with its thick canopy of yellowing leaves and drip ring of very large radius. I had found an English copy of *Swann's Way*—a piece of Marcel Proust's endless *A la recherche du temps perdu*. I'd tried to read it in French in Gillen's senior seminar, but its subtleties were almost beyond my measure. At this point I was perusing it for some of its virtuosic passages of purple prose. Even in English his sentences, rambling artfully unbroken through whole pages, are elegant, the metaphors at times seeming to retrace what they've implied with subtle changes in visual shading, allowing the reader choices.

In one of these remarkable pages we have a call from one child to another over an unspecified distance that seems in a way to become visible. The call is made in the playground park of the Champs-Elysées from a little girl whose name is unknown to us to Gilberte Swann, the fair little nine-year-old beloved of our obsessive narrator: "'Good-bye Gilberte I'm going home now; don't forget we're coming to you this evening after dinner.' The name passed close by me, evoking all the more forcefully the girl whom it labeled . . . forming on its celestial passage . . . a little cloud, delicately coloured, resembling one of those billowing over a Poussin landscape."

A la recherche du temps perdu was published in English as *Remembrance of Things Past,* a title borrowed from Shakespeare's sonnet 30. Its more literal translation would be "To go back and search for things lost in time." In the cases of Proust and other autobiographical novelists, there were frameworks of personal historical truths on which the literary inventions were made.

In this account of my soldiering summer, I've used the recorded time and place facts as my structural form, my painter's visual memory to give it "air" and substance, and my mind's ear to give voices to people. Remembrance is, we must acknowledge, a mixture of memory and invention.

What I did on my duty days is relatively easy to reconstruct, since I do have a list of mission dates and places, even some of the logs;

and as navigator, squadron lead during the last dozen, I know of my actions by recorded facts and through inference. However, my Deenethorpe tour lasted six months, out of which only thirty days, my thirty recorded sorties, are preserved by document. The rest, 150 days, becomes an intriguing and sometimes delightful game of remembrance—a memoir.

Elizabeth and Yokehill Farm were in part documented by drawings, but what she did and the ambience of the place is in the province of my memory, which shifts ever so slightly with each reconsideration. So what I have is a series of speaking images seen in a glass, virtual realities of Elizabeth; *Lispeth* at first because that's how I thought I heard her say her name in English country child's dialect. Then she was Liz, because that was what her "mum" called her; and I, I suppose, called her by all three. Her little person seems to have had certain material qualities and traits that provided starting points for virtual realities within these episodic encounters. A heightened drawing of her would show her hair to be very light colored and a rhythmic tangle. Her eyes were noticeable, and her face mobile and expressive. She was, except on special occasions, barefoot and capable of running in an almost athletic way. Her simple calico dresses were of faded colors with washed-out prints, frugally mended to last out the season. Her older siblings must have been away following the wartime rule that no able hands were wasted. Her father was nowhere to be seen, and I presumed him to be in the army. My image of her mom was rather monochromatic, although she was friendly in a quiet way.

One of my dictionaries lists and defines the several synonyms for memory—*remembrance, recollection, reminiscence, retrospect. Memory* overlaps each of these terms without having all of their specific senses; the plural *memories* sometimes implies a personal, cherished quality. *Remembrance* generally applies to a specific act of recall; in all senses it usually connotes intimate associations. *Recollection* also is limited to a specific instance, which is deliberate and practical rather than sentimental. *Reminiscence* stresses pleasurable, casual recall of intimate matters. *Retrospect* or *retrospection* emphasizes purposeful recall, often accompanied by evaluation.

By these definitions my memories of Elizabeth seem to be a hybrid of remembrance and reminiscence. In any case, they are unusual as inclusions in a memoir devoted primarily to wartime flying adventures. One might even ask why she was given this prominence, although the reasons are not really obscure. Basic among them is that she was symbolic of a future, and every combat soldier hopes to have a future other than death or life as an invalid. I, perhaps more than some, had projected things to come, having graduated from university with more than a notion that an artist's life would be my choice; and further, I would be a teacher and have a family. So Liz was the prototype for a daughter among the children with whom I would someday be blessed. She was conveniently there, and bold for an eight year old going on nine, and she had a good nature in spite of her sometimes solemn expression. Her gift to me was her presence as a fundamental contrast to the German threat to kill or maim.

So when Elizabeth was packed off to Kettering early in September, I did miss her.

20

Ludwigshafen Again

The Germans' will not only to survive as a political entity but to hold on to their ill-gotten gains was shown many times over in the promptness with which they set their expendable slaves to work after the dust from our strategic attacks had settled. Strike photos from the September 3 assault on the I. G. Farben Chemical Works uniformly indicated that our three squadrons had dropped their 500-pounders effectively within a small circular error range; and indeed, all the groups in the 94th Combat Wing had done their jobs well, yet intelligence held that the Enemy had, within a few days, begun to execute his contingency plan to rebuild. But fire is the great cleanser, and an incendiary raid would deprive him of the salvage needed for a running start. But the futility of it all; how many times would it take? War can be painfully redundant. I'm sure, though, the Nazis and a sizable number of their arrogant countrymen felt a similar impatience with the stoic English during the battle of Britain. So, on September 9, the necessary was done. The briefing map again showed the way to Ludwigshafen, and the B-17s were loaded with incendiaries.

My crew did not make the trip. I don't recall whether our 613th was stood-down in normal rotation or whether we as a lead team were not scheduled, an unpredictable rotation system within the squadron. However, Roger Bernard, a Wisconsin native and friend from my class in navigation school and a member of the 612th, did submit to fate that morning and was not seen again at Deenethorpe.

It was reported that his plane took a direct shell strike in the bomb bay, igniting the incendiaries and causing the gas load in the wings to blow the ship into two flaming sections that rolled over and plunged. No bailouts were seen, although the event was closely witnessed from both sides. In virtually every such case we had no news of the individuals who were swallowed in these fiery maelstroms, and as the days and weeks passed we generally assumed that they had joined the great ghost army, though not since Murgatroyd went in at Leipzig had a shoot-down been so jarring to me. You can usually take them in stride; they're part of your ARMA evalution. But this one, even though I'd not witnessed it, was again one of those bright flashes that takes over your consciousness for a while, because through Roger I knew his crew better than many in my own squadron.

Pilot Dave Loughlin seemed almost as young as Roger (who was four years my junior); he was as freckled and boyish as Lindbergh, a Norman Rockwell, yet an able and respected B-17 skipper. Chuck Meredith, his copilot, could have been a slightly older brother, and Ed Sedlak, the bombardier, was blond as a Pole with the cheekbones of a Slavic Czech; pleasantly serious, and who played chess with a cunning that merely toyed with me.

It gave me pause to reflect on all this in a way I seldom did except for a few moments out of the long minutes on a bomb run, to look at the outlandish extravagance of our battle tactics: echelons, the equivalent of rank-and-file in parade review formation, like Civil War flesh-and-blood pawns in the iron enfilade of cannon fire. Even the Brits, with all their moral fiber, went single file, taking evasive action, making the German gunners earn their stripes.

Soon after the end of the war, probably in early September of 1945, I saw Roger a half-block away and across the very broad University Avenue in Madison. Roger Bernard; I could hardly believe it. We had a most happy reunion over some beers on the lakeside terrace.

He had enrolled in engineering at the University of Wisconsin, and I had returned as an instructor in the art department. As you can imagine, I found his story to be a remarkable answer to the question each of us who flew combat asked. What would it be like—the sudden flash that moment when Mars is making a snap decision? Fortunately for Roger, his story has been much longer than the first few seconds of it seemed to promise. In fact at the time of this writing, he is a healthy and prosperous retired engineer with a fine family.

He told me that his plane was at midpoint on its bomb run, beginning to encounter accurate tracking flak with bursts close enough to be heard above the roar of the engines and for the concussions to be felt. The ship was being riddled throughout by jagged pieces of shrapnel, which was at such a place and time normal. After a particularly jarring burst, Technical Sergeant Woody Livingston, his top-turret gunner, called through the intercom that he'd been hit and badly wounded in the thigh and needed help. Roger transferred his oxygen supply tube from its regulator to a "walk-around bottle" and crawled back through the passageway under the pilot deck to the floor of the top-turret, where he found Livingston sitting in a pool of blood. But somehow, while traversing the tunnel, Roger's oxygen tube connection had become detached, and he rapidly lost consciousness. At that moment the roles were reversed. The wounded man, whom Roger had come to help, reconnected the oxygen supply, and Roger regained consciousness just as a shell struck the bomb bay causing a great fire and explosion—which seemed to be the final step into eternity. The front and rear sections of the plane separated at the bulkhead aft of the turret, and the forward structure pitched nose-down throwing Roger so violently against the equipment strewn ceiling that he was again knocked unconscious.

He awakened while falling in a horizontal position on his back with none of the plane debris in sight, nor any other members of the crew. He tried to roll over in order to gauge his altitude but without success, and thought it time to open his chute when he plunged into a wispy cloud layer. His landing in the lower branches of a tree occurred unobserved and without a scratch.

After three days of hiding in wooded hills and four nights of hiking west, he was captured at pistol-point by a young officer. For that he was fortunate, if such a word could be used in that context. We had been warned that the chances of survival if caught by civilians were not at all dependable, and if it became inevitable, it was better to be taken by the military. He was shipped by rail to the northeastern part of Germany and remained in a Stalag Luft until May, when the country was overrun from both directions. Woody Livingston, his wounded top-turret gunner, was the only other crewman from Roger's plane to reach the ground alive, although they did not see each other or know of the other's survival until after the war.

Loughlin, Meredith, and Sedlak were officially listed as killed in action, a term borrowed from the Brits. Happily though, on the other side of the flipped coin, Murgatroyd, Pennoyer, and Elderkin lived to share the hardship of Stalag Luft I at Barth with Roger; but I can only sadly tell you Owen Jorgenson died a soldier's death, KIA.

21

Groesbeek

On September 17, again after a seven-day layoff, we flew a mission that stands out clearly in my memory from briefing to execution. As a matter of fact, it was one of those rare textbook-perfect strikes, and we received a letter of commendation as the lead crew.

The name of the closest town was Groesbeek, in the Netherlands near the German border. It was located five miles southeast of the famous and much fought-over bridge across the Rhine at Nijmegen. But the object of our attack was inside the south edge of a distinctively shaped woods about seven miles southwest of Groesbeek, and was completely hidden.

Lewis and I were given a photo reconnaissance montage and shown exactly what part to strike. We were told with the rest of the crews at briefing that the target of our mission was a Tiger tank repair and maintenance park in this woods, and since the Germans were running out of these particularly dangerous weapons, we probably had a singular opportunity to help our ground friends. Fine. I almost felt enthusiastic and raring to go, but there was one little nagging concern. There were three or four similarly shaped woods in the vicinity as shown on the montage. Also, the IP was one of a cluster of villages. This would take some careful eyeballing.

As missions go, it was not going to be very hazardous or long and fatiguing, but it presented the distinct possibility of making a humiliating blunder. Fortunately, I had had years of visual training in design and in seeing relationships. Also, the weather was clear, exceptionally clear for the Netherlands. No excuse if we failed. Yessir, Colonel Bowman! We would give it our best effort.

We coasted out at Felixstowe, and I used Gee fixes liberally to make sure that our landfall would be right on the mark at a peninsula, actually an island in the estuary of the Maas river, with the ridiculous name Overflakkee. The Netherlands is a complicated little piece of real estate. The Dutch have engineered the land and sea for so long that it's a maze of interconnected islands, channels, rivers, canals, and lakes. And there we were, only sixty miles from the IP with a forty-six-mile-an-hour tailwind giving us a ground speed of 258. I was a little uneasy that we were only fourteen minutes from Hedel on the Maas, which would be the beginning of our bomb run. I could have wished for a head wind. Things were going too fast.

The bomb run would be only twenty-seven miles long on a course of 92 degrees, which would be only about six minutes from the IP. But we were already on a track of 90 degrees, so for all practical purposes we were on the bomb run, and Lewis could start killing rate and course. Fortunately these group-owned lead planes had very finely calibrated instruments. All deviation had been canceled from the Fluxgate compass in the wing tip, so my large circular indicator could be believed to the degree. Our westerly variation was 14 degrees, and with no drift our compass heading was 106 degrees sharp.

Already the check points were coming along right on the money; it was all going so damned fast, but so far so good. I planted myself next to Lewis at his left and kept my pencil point on the detailed pilotage map, with the photo montage in readiness. There was Hedel sliding past under us, and almost incidentally I noticed a few desultory bursts of flak, certainly more than a hundred yards off to the right; must have been amateurs, because we were only at 23,000 feet with such a small target. But, as I said, we were squarely on course, and God damn, there was the woods up ahead right where it should be. Lewis nodded and returned his eye to the sight piece. Bomb doors open? Schlaegel confirmed that they had been open for three or four minutes. That was the right woods, no doubt about it. The shape was a perfect match, and the target area, a long narrow rectangle on the south edge, was all but marked out with a pencil. Lewis was motionless, even his fingers.

"Bombs away," he mumbled, and we both lunged forward on either side of the Norden as far as we could with our helmets off and waited to see the results.

And there it was. The strike rippled through the narrow target to perfection. Jesus, Bowman'll buy us a drink at the club; maybe he'll even promote us.

"Tyger! Tyger! burning bright. In the forests of the night . . ." If those tanks were where they were supposed to be, Heil Hitler!

Okay, Lockhart, turn us around and head back for Overflakkee. No kidding, that's its real name. Lewis and I scrambled up off our bellies, and he had the closest thing to a grin under his ox mask that I'd seen on all of our travels together. Of course, you can only grin with your eyes in that apparatus.

"Got the bastards," he said, curling his gloved thumb and index finger in the "O" signal.

A couple of days later de Jonckheere saw me at the club and came over. "Hey," he said. "You guys sure did a job at Groesbeek. Bowman is hopping pleased. He's going to write you a letter. I saw Lockhart and told him. Haven't seen Lewis; you can tell him."

Sure enough, on September 24 the letter of commendation over Bowman's signature floated down from the blue. It indicated, as I forgot to mention, that the 94th Combat Wing had dispatched four squadrons separately to the target at Groesbeek and that we, the 613th, had achieved superior results. He went on to list all of us from stem to stern, for which I was glad, but of course he listed our guest copilot, a guy by the name of James R. Locher Jr., first.

I continue with a quote from the letter:

An especially laudable feature of your achievement was the fact that the lack of target materials, particularly photos, made the mission at the outset a tough one. Examining the comparatively poor photo which you were given to identify the target, and then observing the splendid results as shown in the bomb-strike photos, it is very gratifying to note the efficiency with which you pinpointed the target. It was an example of precision bombing at its finest. The success which greeted your efforts could only have been attained by thorough pre-mission planning and preparation, smooth team work, and determination.

I'll drink to that. I liked that kind of mission.

Groesbeek had been our twenty-sixth mission, and almost coincidental with our receipt of the letter commending its success, we were awarded the Distinguished Flying Cross. It was not a consequence of that particular achievement, except in a broader sense, but it simply recognized us as survivors in a very dangerous enterprise. Apparently the high command felt that if by the time we had completed twenty-five missions, we were not shot down and killed or taken prisoners or brought home dead aboard battle-ravaged B-17s, or sent away with nervous disorders, we were entitled to a little celebration.

In the same spirit of saying to us, "way to go guys," we were given the Air Medal after each set of five missions that involved gunfire from the enemy. Well, of course, the Germans could always be counted on to shoot at us, so we each had received one of these little blue-and-gold-ribboned beauties and three Oak Leaf Clusters, which signified repeat performances. In addition to all this fruit salad, the whole 401st received the Presidential Unit Citation for extraordinary accuracy in bombing.

The other side of this recognition was the military's tendency to scold and fuss at you like a displeased parent if you made some kind of a blunder, even of a harmless sort. I thought back to the early days when Jardine reminded me of the old army aphorism "never volunteer." Of course we were all volunteers in this business, I'd implied, but he impatiently responded with a you-know-what-I-mean,

"They'll either decorate you, or court-martial you, or both." He was indeed prescient, this friend—not cynical but simply wise. His statement of fact was beyond a cliché in its beautiful symmetry, and soon I was to be the instrument of proof. It could not have been more concise or perfect.

We had just reached the hardstand after a long day's work, anxious to get through interrogation, have a shot or two of Irish whisky, and dig into whatever the cooks had prepared for our pleasure. To help speed the process, I took it upon myself to remove my guns from their Bell adapters, even though I was totally untutored in their deeper mysteries.

I knew that you had to detach the chain-linked line of rounds and pull the charging lever twice to make sure that the chamber was empty, which I thought I had done. However, the unloaded gun went off anyway with an enormous bang that must have been heard for miles over the otherwise peaceful countryside while burying a 50-caliber slug deep in the ground next to the hardstand.

Now, this could have passed as an amusing little incident for Million to kid me about but for the untimely arrival, quite by chance, of the group armament officer. He came roaring up in his jeep yelling, no, almost screaming, "Who cooked off that Goddamned round?"

I was at least given a choice. Through the chain of command, I was asked if I preferred a court-martial, where the merits of my case could be argued, or a decision based on the 104th Article of War, which allowed me to admit my culpability and hope for the best. A court-martial seemed shameful, a disgrace even though unwarranted, so perhaps unwisely I submitted to the 104th Article. It churned through channels forth and back; a reprimand was to be attached to my 201 file, and I was to be fined half my base pay for two months. While all of this was going on I received an Oak Leaf Cluster for my Air Medal and was being evaluated as a potential lead navigator. My patient reader can perhaps detect a bit of irony here, and nod his or her head in agreement with John. Had I learned my lesson about volunteering? No, but I was sure that I would never touch one of those guns again.

22

Forgotten Missions

I've not described, nor do I even remember, some of the missions listed in my file by place names and date. Perhaps it was the canceling effect of redundancy, the lack of specific markers to single them out. Even gut-gripping experiences can, in war, be played over to a point of monotony. The ones that can easily be conjured and retold, though, were unique—Peenemünde for its awesome scale, I might even call it beauty, and a one-time-only privilege of adventure. Others were indelibly marked by a harsher objective standard— with what savagery and yet with what skill did they try to kill us, and by how important and efficacious could I judge our strike to be. Example—being shell-barraged to within an inch of my life at Hamburg on June 20 (my third mission) and then on the way to Berlin the next day, to feel the primitive joy of seeing our enemy's huge oil supply still burning, still sending up great pleasingly shaped clouds of dense black smoke to 30,000 feet. Competing with such basic and perfect battle triumphs as that, our several little tactical raids in nearby France, with the exception of the carpet bombing at Saint-Lô, tended to merge and almost seemed to be a convenience in the business of completing a combat tour.

But then why did Gaggenau, dauntingly deep in the south of Germany, a cold sweaty chore with obvious risks, fail to imprint? It must not have had a significant marker. Perhaps there was only the usual battle damage, and maybe no one that I knew got hurt—and then, of course it had to be compared with Ludwigshafen, where a week later we nearly bought it for a high price, a place that might also have been forgotten except for that single 88 shell that tore through our wing and the calamitous one that zeroed into Roger's bomb bay several days later. We remember even now not only the town name but the object of our attack, the I. G. Farben Chemical Works.

It's easy, of course, to understand why I remember Groesbeek—unique in its challenge to find and hit accurately—not a very hazardous little trip; more of a sporting event you might say, but lavishly praised on paper and attested to by the group commander in a most sincere fashion.

Then Osnabruk two days later simply got buried under the humus of history without a trace; although it was, I think, a strategic rail target located deep enough in northern Germany to get us in trouble. We flew squadron lead and must have done it right, or I'd have had something to remember, and on September 25 we went to Frankfurt, a well-respected place in a highly industrialized area, but, again, I had nothing to mark it with. Eric de Jonckeere might well have been our air commander copilot, although his silence in my (non)memory does not confirm it. We must have, in all probability, done a good job, regardless of the copilot, and returned without bloody losses. Things that were impressive earlier in the summer may have by then become commonplace.

23

Münster

On September 30 we again made Colonel Bowman happy and our squadron CO Eric de Jonckheere proud and caught the attention of the 94th Combat Wing commander, Brigadier General J. K. Lacey.

As I've said, we spent some of our best and most useful efforts in reducing the Enemy's synthetic oil production to a dribble and in depriving him of his ability to move the meager supplies to where they were needed. Large railroad marshaling yards with loaded freight cars were very attractive targets. Münster, in northwestern Germany, was a prime example. It served as a supply transport center for the western front, and we had torn it up several times, but the workers were as persistent as ants in rebuilding. Their zeal testified to its high priority, and after all their hard labor, our P-38s confirmed that it was complete and ready for our attention again. The only problem was that we were having a spate of early autumn bad weather, and Wing was looking to the upcoming fall and winter, with a rather steady layering of heavy cloud cover, so it was time to hone up our H2X through-the-clouds bombing technique. Bill Strong could make himself useful with his crystal ball back there in the room without a view.

At briefing Colonel Bowman virtually promised ten-tenths undercast, and the metro man cheerfully agreed. Our special briefing

Bombing strike photo, railroad marshaling yard, Münster.

emphasized the need for constant communication between our lead team members. Of course. Yes, naturally. This was going to be lots of work, and Eric de Jonckheere was going to be our silent copilot.

After takeoff we were into the clouds at 1,200 feet and were not above them until we reached 16,000, and even then it was pretty murky. Stacking up the formation was hampered by contrails, and I'm sure that our flares were hard to see. Nevertheless, we made the buncher at Lowestoft for coast-out on time. Over the invisible sea I used Gee frequently to verify metro wind on my air plot and found it to be comfortably accurate. The wool pack under us extended ahead to the horizon without a break. Pilotage was not going to be of much use. I was still getting fairly good fixes well into the Netherlands and was transferring them to the pilotage maps for comparison with what Strong saw on his sweep scope. Just fine; the scope picked up shore lines and rivers in sharp contrast; so if he was told where we were, he could keep a very accurate corroboration going with distances and azimuths. We were tracking toward our IP at Meppen about ten miles inside the German border on a prominent north-south river called the Ems, which should show up very well on the mickey. This would give us a fifty-two-mile bomb run on a track of 168 degrees.

Four minutes before our point of turn at Meppen, I asked Russell to start a slow turn to 186 degrees, 14 degrees for mag variation and only 4 for drift; there wasn't much wind. When we'd completed our turn, and were tracking parallel and just east of the river, I began to notice some breaks in the clouds out ahead. It was hard to tell how far they were or how extensive. Lewis nodded and pointed at them.

"Whatdaya think?" he pondered.

"Maybe Providence," I said.

"No shit," he said without humor. "How far are they?"

"Twenty five, thirty miles," I guessed.

He called to Strong. "How far from the target are we?"

"About thirty-two" was the answer.

"Okay," he said in a conversational tone. "We'll go in mickey, but I'll switch to visual if I can."

He was a fast synchronizer, so it began to look like a possibility. I got down at his left with my pilotage map, and he fished out his just-in-case target photos.

In about three minutes Strong yelled, "Twenty-one miles."

The holes were getting much bigger and more extensive. We could see lots of landscape, and there was the Ems curving away to the southeast, with Münster just south of it.

"Range sixteen miles," called Strong.

"Okay, I got it," said Lewis without emphasis.

You could already see the rail lines running into a large elliptical open area, the marshaling yards, and it was dead ahead. Providence, Providence!

Lewis was a statue kneeling at the bomb sight. In spite of the cold he worked with very light gloves, only a subtle movement now and then. I was certain that we had it made. The bomb bay doors were opened more than five minutes ago, and the tracking flak was getting in close now that we were visual for them too.

"Bombs away," and we both dove into the nose bowl. You wanted to count, it seemed to take so long. But there they were, right neat into the elliptical area. "Jesus Christ! We did it again."

"How'd we do?" yelled de Jonckheere.

"You're going to be happy," I told him.

"Come on guys, tell me," he implored.

"It's at least a 90-percenter or better," said Lewis.

We scurried back across the little Dutch acres, and while we were over the Channel de Jonckheere came on the intercom, "Hey, Grilley, how far is it home?" I told him we'd be there in about an hour.

"Can't you make it more direct? Straighten out the bends a little? I gotta go, and my damned relief tube is all froze up."

"You shouldn't have had all that coffee, sir," I offered sympathetically.

But of course the answer to his little inconvenience was the bomb bay, and we'd be down to 12,000 feet in a few minutes, where he'd be free to remove his mask and take a stroll.

At interrogation we got the strike photos posthaste at his influential request, and they were beauties, free of clouds and officially measured at 94 percent, practically unheard of for a switch from H2X to visual. Lewis was a wizard, and our formation had been tight without wobbles.

De Jonckheere was ecstatic. "Look at that," he commanded, slapping the table next to the photos with the back of his fingers. "We sure put the blocks to 'em. Not a carload left, not a friggin' rail that isn't spaghetti, and that's the largest yard in northwestern Germany. Goddamned good going! That's going to look good up at the 94th." He stroked his small black mustache with his index finger. "Buy you a drink down at the club. Don't drink any of that Irish rot-gut. Save room for some twelve-year-old stuff I've got laid away in the back room."

We did exactly what our squadron commander told us to do, but I paced myself and only got a little drunk, without any noticeable ill effects. All in all, it turned out to be as much a social event as a combat mission. The Germans managed some tracking flak that was well

HEADQUARTERS
94TH COMBAT BOMB WING (Hv)
Office of the Commanding General

APO   557
4 October 1944

SUBJECT: Commendation.

TO: Commanding Officer,
       401st Bombardment Group (Hv), APO 557, U. S. Army.

1. Bombing performed by the Low Squadron, 401st Group on the mission to Germany, 30 September 1944, was exceptional and worthy of commendation. Despite extensive cloud coverage, a PFF bomb run was established wherein the Bombardier worked in conjunction with the PFF Navigator to kill rate and deflection accurately. This team work, together with last minute visual corrections on the bombsight by the Bombardier, resulted in a very accurate PFF drop. Strike photos reveal considerable damage to the enemy will ensue. Bombing of this nature indicates that the 401st Group thoroughly understands the use of H2X through clouds technique.

2. I heartily commend the following lead team members and in particular the PFF Navigator and Bombardier for their success on this mission.

Major Eric T. De Jonckheere	Squadron Leader (Co-Pilot)
1st Lt. Russell R. Lockhart	Pilot
2nd Lt. William W. Strong	PFF Navigator
1st Lt. George R. Lewis	Bombardier
1st Lt. Robert L. Grilley	Lead Navigator

J. K. LACEY,
Brigadier General, U. S. A.,
Commanding.

Headquarters, AAF Station 128, APO 557, U.S.Army.   1st Ind.   (G/A/1)
8 October 1944.

TO: Commanding Officer, 613th Bomb Sq (H), 401st Bomb Gp (H), Station.

In forwarding the above commendation from the Wing Commander, I wish to add my personal congratulations and expression of pride for the splendid job that has made such praise justly deserved.

A copy of this correspondence will be placed in the 201 file of each officer concerned.

H. W. BOWMAN,
Colonel, Air Corps,
Commanding.

aimed after we both became visual, but they didn't have enough time, and we'd turned so sharply after the strike that we were all over the place. Six more like that wouldn't be so bad.

When I got back to the hut, I dug out Keats, and flipped it open to "Nightingale." It didn't need a bookmark there anymore.

'Tis not through envy of thy happy lot,
But being too happy in thine happiness, —
That thou, light-winged Dryad of the trees,
In some melodious plot
Of beechen green, and shadows numberless,
Singest of summer in full-throated ease.

Awfully good when you've had a few.

The next day de Jonckheere dropped by our hut and told Russell
and me that Wing was all warm about our job at Münster and that
we were going to get a fancy letter this time from the general. Nice
to have a virtuoso piece applauded by the right people. It was dated
October 4, 1944, and of course it listed, as was only fitting and
proper, Major Eric T. de Jonckheere as our leader. It praised our exceptional teamwork and professionalism under his direction and
went on to say it indicated that the 401st Group (H) thoroughly
understood the use of H2X bombing technique. Colonel Bowman
added his congratulations in an addendum to the letter.

24

Nürnberg

Meanwhile, on October 3, we flew to Nürnberg carrying frag bombs, the kind that were bound in clusters by straps and that became armed when a small charge broke the straps after release. Nobody liked them. You had to tiptoe around the airplane before you got in. I can't remember why we even had them. Maybe it was to crash a party, a reunion of the ghosts of Hitler Youth at the Nazi Stadium in Nürnberg where they used to whoop it up back in 1938.

It was a routine mission. The weather was clear, the flak was so-so; all pretty routine except that we blew a tire on takeoff and veered off the runway. The gear didn't collapse, but we got rather deeply mired down. We all carefully, very carefully got out and tiptoed away. Who knew, maybe those frags were hanging there loose. I didn't envy the armament guys who had to unload them.

Out went the rest of the group while we were carted off to a distant hardstand where a spare B-17 was kept for just such an emergency. It had a load of 250-pounders, which I felt a lot better about. Also it had been gassed up and guns installed. It didn't have a mickey, but no matter; it would be clear all the way. We got a substitute ball gunner, and Strong stayed home. After a brief conference with the Operations officer, we climbed aboard. I think Locher was our guest copilot. My problem was to calculate where the group would be out over the Channel by the time we could get there. I still have the log of that flight, and one entry says, without elaboration, "after Lowestoft, circling to wait for formation."

We landed at 1604 with surprisingly little battle damage for such a prestigious target, and after formalities, I had a quite decent chow at leisure. Except for the blown tire and the fragbombs, that morning, nothing had happened during the day to strike fear in my heart. I caught a jeep ride back to the squadron area and found that I had not been posted, nor had I expected to be. I'd flown no missions back to back as lead.

It was already well into fall at that latitude, but an Indian summer day, if you could call it that in England. Most of the clouds had moved east, and after awhile there would be a red sunset. I'd not been to the Landscape for over a month, not since Lispeth had gone to Kettering to be "happy as a lark." But today the fall colors would be golden, a good way to remember the place, and I was thinking of endings, though perhaps prematurely—there would be five more missions—but the solipsism seemed to have worked its magic so far, and clearly my ARMA had been correctly foretold. Occasionally a crew would go down on its last mission; a bad roll of the dice, but if I shook mine carefully, and spit on them, they'd land right.

I shuffled through the tall yellow grass past Yokehill Farm to get to the hillside where I used to sit and watch the wind waves in the barley, and to be "surprised" by Lispeth. The field had been harvested, but the breeze moved in the autumn weeds, and there was an exceptionally nice sunset. It soon got chilly in the twilight, the kind of chill that comes before you notice it, and suddenly you'd hunch your shoulders and zip up your jacket and think about a scotch at the club.

The next morning I got up at a reasonable hour, it must have been about 7:30, and went down to the mess hall for a leisurely breakfast. There had been a mission sent off early, and some of the stuff was warmed-up leftovers. Porter and John, who still lived with us, had been given the flashlight wake-up call at about 2:00, and Russell was still sacked out, so I was on my own. I seldom saw Lewis on our off days, and we did little socializing.

After breakfast I wrote a letter to my mother. I tried to do that once a week to assure her that I was still of this world, although she would have gotten one of those telegrams from Ulio if I'd have come to a misfortune. The weather was still nice, cool but clear to partly cloudy, so I decided to ride my bike over to an impressive manor house that I'd seen from the air many times. I had heard that the old gentlefolk who lived there were not above letting nice young service men in for a nominal fee.

I bought a packaged lunch and two bottles of beer at the PX and set off. Colonel Bowman ran a more relaxed base than some that I had visited, and officers could leave by flashing their AGO pass. In effect, your time was your own, unless you were scheduled for a mission or practice. But the implication was, of course, that if you were not there when you were expected, you'd be court-martialed.

The place was located about twelve miles or so from Deenethorpe over narrow tree-lined roads. Some fields were still being harvested, and I was reminded of scenes from Thomas Hardy's novels. Once I tried to talk to a farmer, but he paid me not the slightest attention, even when I was almost impolitely persistent.

It was nearly eleven when I got there, so it seemed that I had not followed the most direct route, although, in fact, that would have been practically impossible. The tree-arched drive to the great house was probably a mile long, and I parked my bike a discreet hundred yards from the intimidating portico. Nerve failed me for a frontal assault, and I decided to reconnoiter around to the back. Fortunately we were never allowed off the post without clean full-dress uniform, so I at least felt presentable to gentlefolk.

As I entered an extensive formal garden with large well-sculptured shrubs, I encountered a woman somewhat beyond middle age dressed in a shapeless gray tweed garment. She was rather tall and large boned but noticeably thin. Her hair was a light gray and reminded me of the wig in the Gilbert Stuart portrait of George Washington.

She was pruning a small fruit tree, and when I entered her peripheral vision, she stopped and turned toward me with neither a surprised nor unfriendly look.

"Well, young man, are you out wandering today?" she asked in very upper-class English. "You know that this isn't a public park."

"Yes, ma'am," I answered, trying to suppress any traces of Air Force speech mannerisms. "But I've heard that you do sometimes admit careful visitors to your beautiful house."

"Sometimes we do, if it's for a good reason," she answered, looking me over in some detail.

"You're an American flier from over at Deenethorpe, an officer?"

"Yes, ma'am, Lieutenant Robert Grilley."

"And where do you come from, Lieutenant?"

"From Madison, Wisconsin, ma'am."

"Wisconsin," she repeated slowly, "that's in your midlands."

"Yes, ma'am, in our Midwest," I answered, insisting on a little more accuracy.

"Well, young man, I'm busy at the moment, as you can see. What do you have in mind?"

"Yes, ma'am, I'm sorry to bother you, but I thought perhaps you might have some very fine paintings. Ma'am, do you by any chance happen to have a Constable?"

"Well, Lieutenant, aren't you unusual?" she asked, as if I should elaborate on my unusualness.

I explained that since my arrival in England the previous May, I'd been surprised and delighted to see that England was a wonderful series of Constable paintings.

"Well,"she seemed to begin every sentence with well, as if to express her amazement at how I differed from her generalized image of a young American."In fact we do have a Constable oil sketch, a small one. It's on cardboard and rather loosely done."

"Oh, I like his sketches, ma'am. I think they're some of his best things. They have that marvelous English look. You know, the atmosphere, those rainy greens."

"The painting is in my husband's study, and he's rather engrossed now. And I'm about to change. I'm having my volunteer effort people in for luncheon shortly, for the war effort, you know. Everyone must do his part, as you must certainly know, young man. If you could come back on a Tuesday sometime. Sir Ronald is gone on Tuesdays. He hasn't much patience with visitors, and you could have a few minutes to look at the pictures if he's not engrossed here at home."

She returned to her preoccupation with pruning the tree, but didn't actually ask me to leave.

"Ma'am," I persisted, "do you have other paintings?"

She glanced back at me but not with irritation.

"You are serious, aren't you?" she answered with some show of interest.

"I'll tell Sir Ronald about you. Maybe we could have you to tea sometime when he's not so engrossed. He might like to chat with you. In fact, he has a modest collection: a Landseer of hounds and a George Stubbs of a hunt scene and a portfolio of Hogarth prints. Of course there are the usual portraits of his ancestors. I don't know if you're much into that sort of thing. And then if you're interested in books, he has some early first editions. By the way, do you like Alice?"

"Ma'am?"

"Sir Ronald has some Lewis Carroll first editions and an original Tenniel drawing, *Alice and the Duchess;* he also has one of Carroll's original photographs of Alice Liddell. Like Carroll, Sir Ronald always fancied little girls; oh nothing untoward—kind of thinks of them as flowers. You must take a look at his roses at the other end of the garden on your way out. They won't last too much longer.

Perhaps, if you'd like, you might visit our rector. He's something of an authority on Constable, has some beautiful reproductions. He does have a very nice original John Crome, however. Don't go after Wednesday, though. He does his sermons on Thursdays and Fridays and does parish visits on Saturdays."

"That sounds nice, ma'am," I said, "but I can't plan ahead for such things. I never know when I'll be posted for a mission, but I don't fly quite as often since I began to fly lead. I'll try my luck once more on a Tuesday if one comes up free."

I thanked her as warmly as dignity would permit and took my leave. I walked around the other side of the house, which was very long and architecturally complex, and looked at Sir Ronald's roses, but they were little more than ragged tissues. October had done them in. A little further along I passed some apple trees and picked up three rather decent-looking windfalls. They had a few worm holes, but they polished up nicely. We had plenty of food at our mess, but fresh fruit of any kind was not often available.

It was after twelve when I got back out on the road, and when I'd ridden a mile or so I found a dry grassy bank where I could comfortably stop to eat lunch. There were brown cows grazing in the pasture across the road. How truly bucolic. Maybe I'd have tried my hand at an ode, but shortsightedly I'd forgotten paper and pencil. The day was warming, and a longer trip seemed like a good option.

The quaint crossroad signposts were not very helpful, since I was without a map of any sort, and by 1:30 I was a lost navigator.

I stopped to inquire at country pubs along the way. When I mentioned Deenethorpe, several patrons thought I was kidding. It existed more in name than in substance. I changed my method when it finally dawned on me and asked the way to Kettering. As I was leaving Kettering on the road to Deenethorpe, a flight of B-17s rumbled over; the 401st coming home. While I watched the more distant ones began their peel-off descents and started to drop below the low hills. In an odd sort of way, the sight seemed to be engraving itself in my mind's eye for a future backward glance.

I made it back just in time for postmission chow and saw both Porter and John. They were flying with different crews now—actually

Porter had his own crew—and both reported some troublesome battle damage. They'd gone to Nienburg, and John dusted off his favorite figure of speech to describe the problem. "The flak was so heavy you could get out and walk on it."

They wondered why I had on my necktie and blouse. "You taken to dressing for dinner, Robert?" asked John.

"Went off to visit an important lady today," I told them.

"To improve your mind, no doubt," observed John.

After eating I rode my bike back to the hut to get into something more comfortable and to see if there was any posting for the next morning. I had been back about half an hour sitting in the light of the doorway making a drawing of Sir Ronald's great house from memory when de Jonckheere came rolling up in his jeep.

"Hey, where you been?" he called with an odd look on his face, a funny hint of a smile under his narrow black mustache. "Come on, jump in, I'll buy you a drink."

What was this? We'd always gotten along fine, but in military society he was a couple of cuts above me. In fact, rumor had it that he was about to make light colonel. But he was my CO, so his suggestion was my command. I tossed my drawing pad on the sack and jumped in the jeep just as he spun the tires.

"Lockhart and Lewis are already down at the club having a few," he said, compounding the mystery.

"So, are you telling me something?"

"Yes, I'm telling you something. You're done with your tour," he said with a straight face.

"Whatdaya mean? Come on. Am I getting court-martialed and cashiered?"

"No. I told you, you're done with your tour—finished. You can go home."

"Tell me about it?" I asked.

He pulled a folded mimeographed sheet from his pocket and ordered me to read it.

It flapped around in the wind, and at first I didn't know what I was supposed to be looking at. He slowed down to about forty and took his right hand off the wheel and stabbed at part of the paper with his index finger.

Gradually I pieced it together—General Order Number so and so. To wit: "Lead crews with seven or more credited leads would, after 1 October 1944, be credited with an extra five missions." You get off five missions early is what it was saying. And there my name was, clear as mimeograph ever gets. A jolt of adrenaline hit my unprepared bloodstream, and I yelled something, I don't know what. That night I stayed up late and drank a lot of whiskey. The next day I was pleasantly tired and had a great hangover.

25

After the Last Bomb Run

What I'd called Indian summer ended abruptly, and there was no flying for awhile. A warm front had moved in on a mild southeasterly breeze, and the English fog that came with it dropped conditions to well below instrument takeoff and landing minimums; and there actually were limits, even in those days when making war seemed to be our only raison d'être.

The fact of the matter, though, was that I'd become a bystander, a spectator, since, as Jardine put it, Lewis, Lockhart, and I had been granted a stay and wouldn't be flying in any case. A stay of what? Why, a stay of execution, of course, but he allowed that that might have been a slight exaggeration: "Although, when you think of it in cold numbers," he lectured, "a 3 percent loss-rate per sortie comes to 15 percent for the five missions that you wouldn't have to fly, and that wasn't to be sneezed at; and if Merseburg or Leipzig or BigB or other big jobs were included, the percentage might double." It was a real paradox, quoth he. The more valuable we proved ourselves, the less they were inclined to get extended use out of us. It didn't make sense. Oh Jesus, John, if he was trying to make me feel guilty, it didn't soak in. My euphoria was for a time quite impenetrable. I lounged around eating processed cheese and tinned biscuits from the PX and drinking bottled beer cooled to the fifty-degree room temperature, cool as Keats's grape drink from "the deep delved earth." My sheepskin jacket warded off hypothermia while I skimmed *Wuthering Heights,* which had been lying around since I bought it during the summer to read to Elizabeth.

Liz. I thought of her in her new Kettering guise (happy as a lark), the quintessential English schoolgirl in a pink cardigan and greenish plaid skirt with ribbed white stockings up to the pleated hem and oxfords of heavy brown leather that made her feet look too big. Her wide, well-shaped, rather angular face had gone milk-colored, even a little bluish under the eyes, for lack of sun; but the eyes themselves, a brighter hue in that pale setting remained otherwise unchanged and still completely in charge of her communication system. I got the drawings out for a quick comparison before the image wafted away.

They weren't awfully bad, to use a very English expression I'd picked up, but overly refined. The lines looked coaxed rather than spontaneous and certainly could not have represented Lispeth's easy summer grace. Floating like Botticelli's, they might well have been eleven-year-old Renaissance angels. I could see why Liz and her mum found them beguiling.

Three or four days later, when the fog had risen to become low dark clouds, there was a mission posted for the next morning. My spirits sagged a little, and I did feel uneasy. My friends, most of them, were still in their battle mode; harm was waiting out there to be done to them, and the headless black dwarfs, even the last one, could kill.

Everybody hit the sack early, so I did too, and slept like a farmer. My empathy would be there in the morning, but not very early — and yet, Good God — there it was again, the flashlight in my face, the same deferential nudge and solicitous words. "Sir, it's time to rise."

After a moment of befuddlement I sat up and cuffed the infernal thing out of his hand and lay back on my sheepskin jacket pillow.

"Sorry, sir. I forgot; and by the way, sir, congratulations," was all the fellow said, and that was too much by far. I made no comment, being still half-asleep, while he wandered away to do the job on John and Porter. His memory did serve him better, though, when he came to Russell. I remained in a doze while they dressed, and in an impressive act of courtesy John coughed as quietly as he could and made none of his noisy comments. Porter was his usual considerate self, and a second or two after the door grated shut I sank into a deep slumber. When I woke up, the light coming through the dirty window showed the day to be cloudy bright. It was only a little past seven, so there was still time to get some mission breakfast leftovers if I got a move on.

I came back from biking in the early afternoon in time to watch our B-17s return, and to count them. The last one, number thirty-five, came in on its belly but didn't burn. It landed on the turf, sliding for a half mile in gradual rotation until the plane stopped tail first. That crew and five others had fired red flares during their peel-off, and the ambulances raced away to meet them. The thirty-sixth didn't come back, but word got around that it had bellied in at the seaside station where we'd put down after Ludwigshafen. Porter and John, each with their separate crews, landed without much damage.

Soon after Nürnberg Russell pinned on his captain's bars and got a ride back to the States in a C-54. Rank hath its privileges, but he deserved them. There were many times when I felt a wave of gratitude for his virtuosity, even after something as basic as an instrument takeoff on a short runway, sustained without settling after we'd gotten up out of the false security of ground effect, and for the climb-out in our badly overloaded Bird, up through atmospheric mud in the abusive wake vortex of an invisible B-17 thirty seconds ahead of us. Compared to Russell's line of work, a modern airline pilot eats strawberry cake.

John, finally ruing his self-certain refusal to join us as our lead-team bombardier, flew his remaining seventeen missions as a replacement on a pickup crew, regarding the last five as an affront to his logic. They shouldn't have just sprung this on you after the fact. It should have been a clear contractual arrangement made in advance, out in the open where a guy could make a reasoned decision. "Grilley, you just lucked out."

Porter, somehow at peace with war, was a free agent after he'd flown several deputy leads with us and had been relieved of his seat as Russell's copilot to make way for our air commanders. His first job in transition was to ride tail gun as an officer-observer in the 94th Combat Wing's lead ship; and then he was given his heart's desire, the command of a new B-17 with a crew of survivors for the remainder of his tour.

Lewis and I were at loose ends for the last month of our stay at Deenethorpe. It seemed that the new five-mission credit rule had caught officialdom by surprise, and we were not important enough as individuals to be given special attention; we could be truants for awhile. If we got back to the States too soon, we might be sent off to do unpleasant things in the Pacific. We did give some small further service to the 401st, though, by flying several practice missions up to the Wash to check the proficiency of fledgling lead teams. In general it was true that these bits of arcane knowledge had to be liberally laced with innate judgment and self-possession—some had it and some didn't. All had been schooled and were familiar with the basic tools and math, but how to guess the radius of a formation turn above the clouds and be on time, or how to kill course and rate in the bombsight quickly with or without radar help, seemed in a way to resemble some of the instinctive aspects of bird maneuvers.

Porter finished his tour in late October, about three weeks after I did, and we shipped back together in early November. I don't remember my goodbyes at Deenethorpe in detail, although they must have been warm and deeply felt. There were promises to write, but life goes on helter-skelter, and Americans are not always faithful letter senders.

The war still raged, and the Germans had not yet made their final convulsive rush into the Ardennes, which was to cost thousands of lives on both sides. By any stretch of logic, the huge nonsensical chimera should have been over, but the Nazis seemed to have held their countrymen in some strange thrall, demanding an Armageddon. I had no idea what the coming year of 1945 would show us. The war with Japan had been out of sight and nearly out of mind, an imponderable to me.

26

Back in the U.S.A.

I got back to Madison in mid-November on or about my twenty-fourth birthday, and when my normally demure mother caught sight of me at the station, she let out a whoop heard by everybody meeting the train.

"He flew missions," she cried to passersby, each of whom became an instant friend sharing her happiness. Mother-love can be incandescent.

But I don't think either of us had a very clear idea of what my homecoming would be like, so after our tight hug and automatic small talk, we stepped back to see, as we sometimes can, even in the briefest moment, the state of the other.

She had last seen me as a splendidly tailored young Air Force dandy, with innocence written all over my boyish face. Now I was turning twenty-four and could admit to having caught a glimpse, now and then, through the gates of Hell. I may have had a slightly different cast about the eyes.

It was a tearful scene—a showy display; but even discounting her tears, and considering that she'd be fifty-five in another two weeks, her youthful face as I'd remembered it had aged. She, a World War I widow, had also looked into the gates of Hell, and for a second time.

"They're not going to send you back again are they?" she sniffled.
"No, Mom, they're not."

I'd come home rich. We took a taxi to the best place in Madison and had the finest dinner that wartime shortages could allow, and then some, with a ten-buck tip up front.

All in all, though, I was ready to lighten up. Some new guy had taken my place in Deenethorp, and I wished him luck. My sense of duty had just about run its course, so after a protracted hero's welcome lasting until Christmas, I took the train to the Santa Ana Air Base near Los Angeles for reassignment, with a deep resolve to goof off and mark time for the duration-plus.

When a number of my fellow returnees and I had arrived and unpacked our B-3 bags, the base commander called a convocation to give us some advice.

"These Hollywood babes are going to want to marry you guys," he said with a straight face that brought a roar of self-assured laughter.

"No kidding, guys, it happens all the time; so don't drink too much, and be careful. If you can't be careful and it happens, Officers' Record Section can help you fill out the application forms for dependent allowances."

That was the sum of it. I don't remember another word, no more than a briefing for fair-weather milk runs.

Well, after two weeks I did marry one. She wasn't exactly a Hollywood girl but an art student from Washington University in St. Louis who was visiting her older sister and brother-in-law during her winter break. The brother-in-law was at the time a famous artist, an American Degas or Renoir whom I contrived to meet almost immediately.

The combat ribbons and wings on my tunic and my all-but-overly-confident air opened the door for me, and the artist was cordial beyond my expectations. Over several martinis we sat for a whole afternoon discussing French painting, and when I rose to leave he assured me that I was more than welcome to stay for dinner. Much later that evening, he warmly invited me to come back during my stay in Santa Ana to draw in his studio, with the cute young sister-in-law as a model. That's how things could be in time of war.

After the mentioned two weeks, during which everything went swimmingly, I got my orders to leave. When I told the cute little sister-in-law, I asked playfully if she'd like to come along. She replied that of course she couldn't; she was about to return to school. So I said, "It's been real nice. Let's keep in touch."

When I got back to base I packed my B-3 bag, and while I was checking out a chute at the operations office and filling out the manifest, a smirking sergeant called, "Hey, lootenant, some babe wants you on the phone."

You guessed it, or rather, I already told you. I got a delay in route, and we were married by one of the lady judges of Los Angeles County. She gave us a kind yet stern lecture about the solemnity of our action and hoped we'd bear that in mind for many years to come.

We took a sleeper to the Gulf Coast of Texas and prepared to continue wasting more government time and money. We rented a small, virtually unfurnished house in Texas City from which I commuted to Ellington Field near Houston with a neighbor, a captain in charge of Officers' Record Section. At Ellington they presumed to give me a refresher course in navigation and meteorology, but there, in fact, my main enterprise would be to buzz back and forth between Georgia and New Mexico to catch up on my flight pay. Flying was still considered inherently hazardous, even when no one was shooting at you, which entitled you to extra compensation. It fit right into my plans to goof off.

I whiled away much of the spring getting fat and rich. I knew as much about navigation as I'd ever need to know, and the weather guys were welcome to their metro.

At Ellington our lives seemed to be on hold; one day like the next, but things in the outside world were moving. New pages were being filled and turned in the history books. FDR was dead and the Germans had gone belly-up. The Russians were our allies, but maybe not. Who knew? And the war with Japan, as it had been, was only in my peripheral vision. I shrugged. So far, so good. I had been to Merseburg, Leipzig, and Berlin over and over, each with more than a thousand heavy guns, and here I was without a scratch, healthy as a young farm boy. It was almost indecent. I'd gone through the war and hadn't suffered.

One afternoon while I was having a drink at the club with an old squadron buddy, my neighbor, the captain in charge of Officers' Records Section, stopped by and put his hand on my shoulder.

"Hey Grilley, yer from Madison, Wisconsin. Right? Oh man, do I have a deal for you."

He sat down and munched a couple of my potato chips and sipped his beer. "What a deal. It came in just before we closed. Lucky I spotted it for you, and you get flying pay with it."

So I became the newly appointed public relations officer at Truax Field, the largest radio training school in the Air Force. We did the paperwork the next morning, and I was on the job in Madison four days later.

The brigadier general CO assumed that, since I was a university grad, I could write coherent sentences (news releases to the Madison newspapers) and was socially tactful enough to take care of such delicate matters as hosting bereaved parents who came to be awarded their sons' posthumous combat medals. It was a nine-to-three job with just enough pointless flying to earn my flight pay.

As you can imagine, I lost no time visiting the old folks in charge of the UW art department, who fondly remembered me, and of course, to let them know I'd be available soon after VJ Day.

That's exactly how it turned out, and I started my forty-two years of tenure, right after that miraculous moment in time. Many of my first students were there on the GI Bill.

My first work of art was a little English landscape with a B-17 on landing approach from which a red flare arches back in a graceful

Porter Ham and Robert Grilley, at 401st reunion, Norfolk, Virginia, September 1992.

curve. Its thin trace of scarlet is a fine accent against the dramatic sky, but to the medics its message was that there were wounded on board. I called the picture *Return from Berlin.*

My often tempestuous first marriage produced three much-loved children, a daughter and two sons. But after twenty-three years of war and peace, my wife took leave and went off to Mexico with one of my most illustrious colleagues to get a divorce and marry him.

But, all's well that ends well, and after six years or so of somewhat aimless and at times bemused bachelorhood, I met and married a beautiful, extremely accomplished Japanese scientist who was here first on a research fellowship and then a tenured professorship.

We have a delightful daughter, as is often the case with a Caucasian and Asian mix, and since I was an older-than-usual daddy, I had more discretionary time to spend with her—for art and flying our souped-up Cherokee, often as far as western Montana to visit John Jardine, and to explore the high Rockies from the air and on foot.

She's also the perfect mother's daughter, a medical student with what seems to be a heritable propensity for research.

The years have been remarkably slow to injure me, and if anything, I've done my best work since middle age. As I'd hoped, I became an exceptionally skillful, even inspired, painter, and I'm quite prepared to say that, had I been born at a much earlier date, I might well have made a good living as an old master.

Appendix A: American Strategic Bombing

Appendix B: Missions

Appendix C: Robert Grilley's
Military Decorations

Appendix A:
American Strategic
Bombing

After looking at the missions specifically, it's worth considering the larger question of what the American strategic bombing campaign in Germany was attempting to do, how it fit into the overall effort to bring about a total unconditional defeat of the Nazi dominion.

Germany's war plans and actions from long before the first shots were fired were based on an unprecedented industrial capacity for the production of arms, munitions, fuel, and transportation. Never before had war been so extensively planned on the ability of fighting machines as well as on soldiers. The new concept of mechanized warfare was at first overwhelming. With Poland as a practice field, and then with France as the big game, won by a huge score, the Germans seemed invincible. After driving the remnants of the British Expeditionary Forces into the Channel at Dunkirk, Hitler's plans seemed to be on the verge of total success.

At that point it seemed to the Germans that England could be weakened to a point where invasion might be accomplished with ease by heavily bombing the cities. Supposedly the people would be terrorized into submission, and the Nazi triumph would be complete.

Well, as we all know, it did not work. The Spitfires and Hurricanes flying with radar direction caused the German bombing campaign to fall far short of its objective, and the English people suffered through it with increasing anger and resolve to hold the fort. It finally wound down to an impasse, and, although they did not realize it at the time, we can, in retrospect, see that the Germans lost the war when they lost their momentum.

Time ran out, and the entry of the Americans into the war, together with the disastrous struggle with the Soviets, sealed the outcome, but the Germans seemed to demand their final execution. Hitler was not about to fall on his sword, and hundreds of thousands more lives were to be sacrificed. Germany was still a vigorous industrial giant with a huge military. The Luftwaffe and the mechanized armies were still awesome, manned by tough veterans, and the obedient German civilians were ready to carry on to wherever. So now that we, the Allies, had this vicious animal at bay, how were we to pull his fangs and get him into a cage?

The Dunkirk disaster had left the remnants of the British Army impotent and ill equipped (probably more so than Hitler knew), and the long wait for the American mobilization and the products of our manufacturing magic began. Although they had some minor success in the desert of North Africa, the British could do little else but launch a campaign of bombing against Germany. They had developed three heavy four-engine bombers, the Sterling, the Halifax, and the Lancaster, which were designed as prodigious load carriers, intended to fly their missions at night relatively free from fighter attacks. Although it was clear that the German bombing of English cities had failed in its purpose, the British strategy was directed to the same idea: pound, pulverize, and burn German cities to the ground and terrorize and kill the civilian population, all of this on a scale vastly greater than the Germans were able to visit on the English targets. They pursued this approach from 1942 throughout the rest of the war, and such famous firestorms as were experienced by Hamburg, Dresden, and many other cities are part of history.

The method that they employed was remarkably simple in concept. Send flare-dropping pathfinder planes to mark the target areas, followed by bombers flying individually rather than in formation to dump saturation loads of high explosives and incendiary devices. The theory was that if you drop enough bombs you are bound to hit something.

In contrast, even on a theoretical basis in the mid-1930s, and under the constraints of the Great Depression budget, the U.S. Army Air Corps was carrying on research and development of a long-range bomber capable of accurate bombing from very high altitudes. It was to be able to deliver a heavy load over a long distance and to strike a highly specific target with "pinpoint" precision. In a competition among Douglas, Boeing, and Martin, Boeing presented by far the boldest and most innovative design. It was the largest, the only one with four engines, and, as an aircraft, strikingly beautiful; it was the prototype of what was to become the B-17. Of course its ultimate promise of great accuracy was predicated on two things: the ability to penetrate the airspace of a vigorously hostile enemy in the full light of day, and in so doing defend itself from fighters, and to have a means of aiming the bombs from this fast-moving, high-flying aircraft.

During its subsequent development into a wartime dreadnought, the B-17 acquired an impressive array of thirteen .50-caliber machine guns, including three power turrets, thus warranting the name Flying Fortress. But its proclaimed ability to "drop a bomb in a pickle barrel from 25,000 feet" was dependent entirely on its highly secret Norden bombsight. This gyro-stabilized device was, in a precomputer age, a uniquely precise instrument, a mathematical wonder; and while the above-mentioned claim for its magic was slightly exaggerated, the combination of this great airplane and the Norden bombsight provided the first opportunity to attack truly strategic military targets, as compared to heavy campaigns of urban mass destruction.

At first the British were unimpressed with our proposal for daylight bombing, saying that only our neophyte innocence kept us from realizing that the German fighters and flak gunners would eat us alive. They counterproposed that we tool up and build an armada of Lancasters and follow their lead in night bombing the Third Reich into a glowing pile of cinders. However, after a combination of diplomacy and arm twisting, our Eighth Air Force was allowed to settle on

English soil. The clichéd term *fledgling* is overused, but in this case it was appropriate. Trial and error was costly; before we had the P-51s to scourge the Me-109s and the FW-190s over the length and breadth of their homeland, our fledgling bomb groups paid a dear price.

But even after the Mustangs began to overpower the Luftwaffe fighters, our Eighth Air Force Bomber Command costs continued to be very high. Altogether, between August 1942 and May 1945, 4,754 B-17 Flying Fortresses and 2,112 B-24 Liberators were lost. By early 1944 flak was taking an ever-increasing toll. The Germans assigned more than two million men to their antiaircraft defense and devoted between 30 and 40 percent of their ammunition production to that purpose.

In the postwar period the word *flak* entered the English lexicon primarily in its figurative sense. Thus, one might say that a certain politician took some heavy flak for his unpopular proposal. But of course in the context of this narrative, its frequent use refers to the real thing, an extremely lethal form of aerial artillery capable of firing large explosive shells more than five miles vertically with remarkable accuracy and with altitude fusing. Actually, FLAK is a German acronym reduced from one of their line-filling compound words, *Fliegerabwehrkanonen,* which translates as "flyer defense cannons." The most widely used type was a more powerful adaptation of their general-purpose 88 mm field gun, and in its ultimate form flak was a version of the more violent 105 mm piece, with an explosive shell length of 470 mm. These would blossom into huge black explosions hurling jagged shrapnel, deadly at a hundred yards or more.

However, as the reader can well appreciate, our losses could not primarily be counted in downed aircraft. Our enormous production ability could replace them at a prodigious rate. The real losses were human. The Eighth suffered 46,456 casualties, not counting prisoners. Often our bombers, looking to be intact, would bring back dead and wounded, while others fell as ashes on German soil or in the

North Sea. The little painting reproduced on this book's cover shows a red flare arching back from the descending B-17, indicating wounded on board.

This heavy attrition caused the breakup of a number of crews, and there were many spares left suspended in time until they could be reassigned as replacements. In many instances whole new crews were formed from this pool of survivors.

Also, there was the very disturbing problem of stress-induced breakdowns. In less severe cases it was called combat fatigue, and a brief period spent at a rest and recreation facility might restore the damaged psyche, but some were irretrievable and had to be sent back to the States.

The Air Force had, in fact, anticipated this eventuality, and devised a screening system called ARMA or Aptitude Rating for Military Aeronautics. So, during our sorting-out period of testing prior to Aviation Cadet training, we were each given an individual exam and interview by two psychologists, a half an hour or so of informal conversation skillfully manipulated to draw out our innermost feelings and emotions. This may have seemed rather arbitrary, but since there was a huge backlog of applicants, the decision makers could afford to be extravagant in their choices, and an astonishing number were rejected, including some conspicuously macho types.

In retrospect, I've always been glad that we elected the strategy of striking at Germany's arms and fuel production and at their transportation infrastructure, rather than following the British lead of saturation-bombing urban areas. More than 600,000 German civilians were killed, including some 120,000 children, in most cases by the less discrete methods of the RAF Bomber Command. We were not without guilt; but by and large we stuck to our avowed intent, and many of the Nazi elite in unison with their top brass sorrowfully testified to the efficacy of the bitter medicine that we fed them. Joseph Goebbels, perhaps Hitler's most trusted theoretician, lamented in his diary two months before his death that the Americans roamed at will over Germany, and it was of little use to have fighters with no fuel to fly them. Also, very much to the point, top Luftwaffe general Karl Bodenschatz said, "I am very much impressed by the accuracy of the American daylight bombing, which really concentrated on military targets and factories, to the exclusion of others."

What an extraordinary compliment.

Appendix B:
Missions

June	14	Paris Le Bourget
	17	Monchy-Breton
	20	Hamburg
	21	Berlin
	22	Frevent
	25	Montbartier
July	6	Renascure
	7	Leipzig
	12	Munich
	16	Munich
	20	Leipzig
	24	Saint-Lô
	25	Saint-Lô
	28	Merseburg
	29	Merseburg
	31	Munich
August	1	Chartres
	5	Nienburg
	8	Hautmesnil
	18	Yvoir
	25	Peenemünde
	27	Berlin
September	3	Ludwigshaven
	10	Gaggenau
	13	Wesel

	17	Groesbeek
	19	Osnabrük
	25	Frankfurt
	30	Münster
October	3	Nürnburg

Appendix C:
Robert Grilley's
Military
Decorations

Distinguished Flying Cross
Air Medal and three Oak Leaf Clusters
Presidential Unit Citation
ETO with two Bronze Battle Stars